T0033425

LITTLE HOUSE
LIFE HACKS

LESSONS FOR THE MODERN PIONEER FROM
LAURA INGALLS WILDER'S PRAIRIE

ANGIE BAILEY AND SUSIE SHUBERT
ILLUSTRATED BY LAUREN MORTIMER

RUNNING PRESS
PHILADELPHIA

Running Press
Hachette Book Group
1290 Avenue of the Americas, New York, NY 10104
www.runningpress.com   @Running_Press

Printed in China

First Edition: August 2023

Published by Running Press, an imprint of Perseus Books, LLC, a subsidiary of Hachette Book Group, Inc. The Running Press name and logo are trademarks of the Hachette Book Group.

The Hachette Speakers Bureau provides a wide range of authors for speaking events. To find out more, go to www.hachettespeakersbureau.com or email HachetteSpeakers@hbgusa.com.

Running Press books may be purchased in bulk for business, educational, or promotional use. For more information, please contact your local bookseller or the Hachette Book Group Special Markets Department at Special.Markets@hbgusa.com.

Print book cover and interior design by Frances J. Soo Ping Chow

Library of Congress Cataloging-in-Publication Data:
Names: Bailey, Angie, author. | Shubert, Susie, author. Title: Little House life hacks: lessons for the modern pioneer from Laura Ingalls Wilder's prairie / Angie Bailey and Susie Shubert. Description: First edition. | Philadelphia: Running Press, 2023. Identifiers: LCCN 2022036113 | ISBN 9780762481996 (hardcover) | ISBN 9780762482009 (ebook) Subjects: LCSH: Life skills. | Little house on the prairie (Television program)—Influence. | Wilder, Laura Ingalls, 1867–1957—Influence. | Wilder, Laura Ingalls, 1867–1957. Little house on the prairie. Classification: LCC HQ2037 .B35 2023 | DDC 158.1—dc23/eng/20220819 LC record available at https://lccn.loc.gov/2022036113

ISBNs: 978-0-7624-8199-6 (hardcover), 978-0-7624-8200-9 (ebook)

APS

10 9 8 7 6 5 4 3 2 1

CONTENTS

AUTHORS' NOTE

When the global pandemic took hold at the beginning of 2020, we reacted as most people did: washing our hands incessantly, scouring the aisles for antibacterial wipes and toilet paper, eating and cocktailing our way to comfort, and plopping ourselves in front of the TV for mind-numbing entertainment. Thank goodness for streaming episodes of *Little House on the Prairie*! Not long after we became reacquainted with our pioneer friends and the show's heartfelt themes, we realized the wisdom gleaned from the story lines was timeless enough to apply to the circumstances we found ourselves in, and we dove eagerly into all nine seasons and later the entire book series. Stepping back in time to revisit the *Little House* community was sheer delight. We had such fond memories of both the books and the television series, which were a big part of our childhoods. (Susie may have even had a prairie-style sleeping cap of her own, and Angie's braided pigtails looked suspiciously similar to Half Pint's.)

We were really looking forward to diving into the kitschy bliss that was 1970s and '80s television: corny life lessons, teary drama, and Michael Landon's bare, sweaty chest. But rereading the books also brought back our appreciation of their enduring tales of life as a struggling pioneer in the 1800s; we fell in love with little Laura and the entire family all over again.

Although our modern life seems so removed from what was portrayed through Laura's words or a Hollywood camera lens, the desire to live a life of happiness, community, fulfillment, and purpose is something we as a people have always strived for.

Contrary to the prime-time episodes' dramas, which were usually tied up with a nice burlap bow, real life as a pioneer was a constant struggle and anything but easy. As we were heading into a harsh Minneapolis winter during our modern-day plague, we would often meet to write in the well-ventilated safety of Susie's screened porch (which was probably at least twenty degrees warmer than Pa's town building on a balmy winter's day in De Smet, South Dakota), shivering away as we revisited the prairie. And yes, we sometimes complained about the cold, but considering what our counterparts went through in the Ingalls family's time—not to mention what some of our contemporaries were experiencing on the front lines of the pandemic—it was a huge reality check.

As difficult as it was to adjust to the "new normal," both in coworking and in living life in general, there was a sort of strange magic to that time that helped us better embody the spirit of the Ingalls family. And it wasn't just us; since the recession of 2007, the desire to live more minimally and simply seemed to be a rising trend that COVID-19 just brought that much closer to home.

Even with our modern conveniences, and perhaps because of them, we collectively yearn for some pioneer simplicity. How a hot meal with the family (blood kin or chosen) around the table was eaten with appreciation and reverence. The way children were overjoyed when given a pair of handmade mittens or a single piece of candy. How everyone knew their neighbors, and they could typically be depended on for a hand and a smile. How the idea of limited choices or options can sometimes feel easier, and putting in a hard day's work to simply fall into bed when the sun goes down seems like an uncomplicated relief.

We're a couple of realistic gals, and we're pretty darn grateful for our own modern conveniences. (Thank goodness for online streaming, modern medicine, and coffee around every corner!) We don't want to give them up or feel bad for using and enjoying them. But why can't we have it all? Or strive to, at least. How do we take the simple ideals and down-to-earth sensibilities of *Little House on the Prairie* and sprinkle a little of that Pa Ingalls wisdom and wit into our contemporary lives? That was our goal with this book. To enhance *your* experience, we encourage self-reflection throughout the chapters, so we recommend keeping a journal or notebook handy as you read.

It must be said that many moments in both the *Little House* books and show demonstrated how much we needed to grow and expand as a people; we still have a long way to go, but thankfully, outlooks on diversity, inclusion, and respect for women have improved since then and hopefully continue to progress. We have tried to expand on this and hope that's clear in the examples we have given throughout the book. We can't erase history, and we believe it's important not to; that's how we learn and grow. We can always do better, and we hope our little book inspires you to do so in all the areas of your life.

We also hope it motivates you to think and try new things and provides you with the peace of a little more simplicity, a feeling of purpose, and the sweet and happy vibe that's so often felt in *Little House on the Prairie*.

INTRODUCTION

Picture this: In the middle of an economic downturn, people lose their traditional jobs and find themselves immersed in the fickle gig economy; home cooking and baking are mainstays in meal preparation; families make difficult choices about how they're going to spend the little money they have; a pandemic spreads across the nation; clever resourcefulness takes a front-row seat and people tackle DIYs with newfound aplomb; mental illness and addiction affect large numbers of vulnerable people; individuals find comfort and love in unconventional family structures; environmental disasters destroy lives, homes, and businesses; people seek ways to live sustainably; people of color experience racism at the hands of law enforcement; protests and unrest mount in the face of increasing inequity; bullying and mobbing ruin lives and social standing; arts, crafts, and creative games become more prominent as people spend more time at home; women seek independence and speak out against sexism and discrimination despite facing backlash; and individuals struggle with toxic relationships. Phew!

Sounds like a pretty accurate description of what we've been collectively living through, right? Well, hold your horses, folks, because these challenges are *also* straight out of the book series and cult classic television show *Little House on the Prairie*, which depicted life on the 1800s American frontier and starred the Ingalls family living in the newly settled Midwest.

Our new normal is forcing many of us to become twenty-first-century pioneers. With our increasingly complicated lives, we find ourselves comforted by the basics and determined to learn new skills either by choice or necessity.

I AM BEGINNING TO LEARN THAT IT IS THE SWEET, SIMPLE THINGS OF LIFE WHICH ARE THE REAL ONES AFTER ALL.
—LAURA INGALLS WILDER

As young Gen X kids, we devoured the biographical series of books that began with *Little House in the Big Woods* (still popular among youngsters today) and were hooked on the television series that made those stories and so much more come to life. Entire families sat in their living rooms or wood-paneled basements, shacking up with the Ingalls family every Monday or Wednesday night for almost ten years in the 1970s and '80s. We worried when Pa's crops got destroyed in a hailstorm, cried (and had nightmares!) when Mary went blind, cheered when Laura punched that bratty Nellie Oleson, and felt the warm fuzzy glow as the family loved one another fiercely through it all.

As we grew into latchkey teens, we spent many afternoons alone in front of television reruns, and over time, we started to feel like part of the small screen families with which we shared our homes. Although both real and imagined pioneer life were fraught with trials and tribulations—one failed crop could cause the devastating loss of income for an entire year—*Little House on the Prairie* was a feel-good favorite that comforted us, made us laugh, and showed us that we could stand up to that playground bully or survive a parent losing a job and that "doing unto others" really was the golden rule.

Humans tend to look back at older times with longing and a belief that life in the past was simpler and easier to deal with, when in reality, it was as complicated as our own. The show's perfect formula, where a challenge is introduced, dealt with, and generally all tied up with a heartfelt lesson in an hour's time, has never been close to reality either, of course. But the lessons on coping, creativity, and resourcefulness from the show and the books can help us navigate today's world with determination, perseverance, humility, and gratitude. The Ingalls family members are the perfect reminders of what's most important: love, family, community, and integrity. And apple fritters. Eat the apple fritters.

In the pages of *Little House Life Hacks*, we (a humor writer and a life coach) have gathered timeless gems of sage wisdom from the much-cherished book series first published in the 1930s and the show that originally ran from 1974 to 1983. The latter iconic series still lives on in syndication and through popular streaming providers—as well as in our hearts—and the former finds new fans in young bookworms every year.

Our Ingalls-inspired practical advice for home, work, and relationships includes lessons in preparation and resilience when best-laid plans are unexpectedly upheaved, doing the most with what you've got, tackling dreaded tasks with creativity and intention, and realizing that you actually have the power of choice in most of your daily doings. And as the world feels more harried and disconnected, we find ourselves wanting to reconnect with family, nature, and, ultimately, ourselves.

Our hope with this book is that, in addition to supplying a lovely nostalgia factor and a healthy dose of kitschy delight, we provide you with meaningful tidbits of inspiration for infusing more balance, wellness, and fun into the many aspects of your life. Seriously, who doesn't need timeless tips for creating a more meaningful love life à la Ma and Pa Ingalls? Who better to demonstrate how to manage an overwhelming workload in the face of stormy weather than Pa Ingalls? Who couldn't use fresh angles for maneuvering Nellie Oleson–style relationships while keeping your cool, maintaining integrity, and not stress-eating an entire sleeve of Thin Mints?

Like the pioneers experienced, life often throws a raging river in our path that threatens to slow us down or change our course, but armed with wisdom, tenacity, and a strong will, we can get through it and are often pleasantly surprised at the newfound opportunities that the obstacle has opened for us.

So tie on your bonnets, pull up your boots, and hop into our covered wagon. Let's stake our claim on some *Little House* life hacks.

BUT THE REAL THINGS HAVEN'T CHANGED. IT IS STILL BEST
TO BE HONEST AND TRUTHFUL; TO MAKE THE MOST OF
WHAT WE HAVE; TO BE HAPPY WITH SIMPLE PLEASURES AND TO BE
CHEERFUL AND HAVE COURAGE WHEN THINGS GO WRONG.
—LAURA INGALLS WILDER

MEET THE INGALLS FAMILY AND NEIGHBORS

YOU'RE NEVER ALONE, HALF PINT, NOT EVER.
—PA INGALLS
SEASON 8 • EPISODE 17 • "DAYS OF SUNSHINE,
DAYS OF SHADOW, PART I"

L aura Ingalls Wilder wrote her books based on and
around the events and people of her real life. The television series remained true to the main characters of
Laura's family, but it took plenty of liberties with friends and
townspeople. Although we've delved into both the books and

the show for inspiration, many of our references to specific people are taken from our prime-time pals. For those of you who didn't sit down in front of the TV every Monday night from 1974 to 1983 for your weekly *Little House* fix, don't remember much about the characters, or simply don't have a clue about the show, don't you fret! Like your favorite wagon, we've got you covered. We couldn't possibly name every character that showed up in the book series or all nine seasons (wait, there were nine seasons?) of the show, but here we list the ones that are most mentioned in this book.

CHARLES (PA) INGALLS: Pa was the glue that held the *Little House* together. He was the ultimate example of a hard-workin' man who pushed through obstacles with a twinkle and a tear in his eye. It would seem the weirdly frequent sight of his naked torso on television contributed to his stellar work ethic—you may or may not want to try this technique at home.

As a father to his ever-growing family, he always had enough love and time to give. As a husband, he was ever attentive and often willing to put aside his manly pride to help his wife, Caroline, around the house. Charles tended to see the best in everyone, so you couldn't have asked for a better friend. He did whatever he could to provide for his family and was never too proud to find work where he could when there was no grain to harvest or lumber to saw at the mill. Chock-full of wisdom and integrity, Pa had a can-do attitude and love of family and community that were the gold standard in Walnut Grove. More than likely, men of the 1970s and '80s both loathed and respected him; his was a hard act to follow.

CAROLINE (MA) INGALLS: Ma Ingalls was a complicated woman. As the show began, she seemed a bit cold and strict, but as time went on, she softened and became the Ma we knew and loved. Pa couldn't have worked half his magic without Ma behind the scenes sewing clothing, frying chicken, scrubbing floors, and making sure everyone did their chores. She may have lived in a time when women had certain boundaries and were seen as the "weaker sex," but that never stopped her from getting out there and plowing the field, telling off Mrs. Oleson, and even schooling Charles a time or two. When times were lean, she got a job outside the home, in addition to all that she was doing there. Of course, Ma was also the quintessential cook and baker; Pa couldn't get enough of her apple fritters, and she could crack an egg one-handed without getting one bit of shell in the bowl. Despite the piety and petticoats, she was a fierce suffragette. She led the town's wives in a women's rights strike. Ma had the perfect combination of sweetness and strength that any modern woman can admire.

MARY INGALLS: The eldest of the Ingalls brood, do-gooder Mary never met a rule she couldn't follow. She loved nothing more than to read a good book and study hard for her straight As. She was a good big sister and always had Laura's back. Sadly, at age fifteen, she started having vision trouble, and before long, she woke up blind, terrifying young fans of the show. Mary learned to thrive despite this unfortunate event, and although we never learned of a husband in the book series (in fact, the real Mary never married), on the show, she opened a school for the blind with her husband, Adam. She and Adam lived through hard times, losing one child to miscarriage and another in a fire.

LAURA (HALF PINT) INGALLS: Laura Ingalls was curious, bold, and caring; she was the friend you always wanted in grade school. She was a sassy, justice-seeking tomboy who would rather go fishing than learn the traditional role of the good pioneer wife. She stood up for her friends and herself against that "mean ol' Nellie Oleson." She loved to exercise her independence, but always with the best of intentions, a kind heart, and a sense of wonder. She grew up to become a teacher, and married the man of her dreams, Almanzo (Manly) Wilder, whom she had a crush on since childhood in the show. In the books, he was the one who had to work his way into *her* heart! As was common in the pioneer era, Laura and Manly dealt with hard times, sickness, and death in their family. All the while, Laura kept her spark.

CARRIE INGALLS: When the series began, Carrie was the youngest Ingalls sibling. Always looking up to her older sisters, she often felt left out of the "big girl" activities. Most of the show's

fans were thankful when she finally graduated from baby bab-
ble and stopped talking with food in her mouth.

ALBERT (QUINN) INGALLS: Once an orphaned rapscallion living by
his wits, Albert met the Ingalls family during their short-lived
stint in the bustling fictitious town of Winoka, Minnesota.
Despite his wily ways, he stole their hearts and eventually
returned to Walnut Grove with the family to become their
adopted son. Albert was not a part of the real Ingalls family,
but with his big brown eyes and penchant for drug-induced
drama in the latter years, we're so glad he was added into
the show!

ADDITIONAL INGALLS CHILDREN: The family ultimately expanded
to include the birth of Grace and, only on the show, the adoptions of later siblings Cassandra and James, who lost their
parents in a runaway wagon accident (like you do). There usually was plenty of rabbit stew to go around.

MEET THE NEIGHBORS

LAURA THOUGHT OF MA'S SAYING,
"IT TAKES ALL KINDS OF PEOPLE TO MAKE A WORLD."
—LAURA INGALLS
LITTLE TOWN ON THE PRAIRIE

ISAIAH EDWARDS: Charles's longtime friend Isaiah was a diamond in the rough who won over the community with his good heart, helpful spirit, and a never-ending chorus of "Old Dan Tucker." Described as "tall and skinny," readers were introduced to him in *Little House in the Big Woods*. On the television series, a burlier Isaiah found love in moonshine and postmistress Grace Snider. They got married and adopted orphaned siblings John Jr., Carl, and Alicia.

NELS AND HARRIET OLESON: In *On the Banks of Plum Creek*, William and Margaret Owens were the owners of the local mercantile and had children Nellie and Willie. Although the long-suffering television version of Nels was a down-to-earth fellow, he married snooty wannabe socialite Harriet, and together they raised a couple of ungrateful kids who didn't appreciate the value of a dollar.

NELLIE OLESON: The ultimate mean girl of the series, Nellie was a character we all loved to hate and was actually a combination of a few different girls in the real Laura Ingalls's life. Nellie's bullying typically backfired on her, which pleased Laura (and us) to no end. Eventually, she met her match (and her love) in restaurant consultant Percival. They settled down in New York and had a family of their own.

WILLIE OLESON: As Nellie's younger brother and sidekick, Willie could usually be found in the outhouse or causing some sort of trouble. (The real Willie wasn't mentioned much in the book, so we don't know about his bathroom habits.) The youngest Oleson's behavior often resulted in standing in the school-room corner or staying after class to clean the chalkboards.

NANCY OLESON: After Nellie married and moved away, Harriet found herself lost without a miserable daughter to spoil. Enter Nancy Oleson, the spitting image of Nellie in both look and demeanor. As predicted, no one in town rejoiced in this addition to the Oleson family—and luckily for the real Oleson family, there was no IRL Nancy.

DOC BAKER: On the show, Hiram Baker was the go-to medical professional. He was also a trained veterinarian treating both the humans and the animals of Walnut Grove with loving care, pliers in hand.

REVEREND ALDEN: TV Walnut Grove's spiritual leader and voice of reason. The reverend was approachable and open-minded, and always had words of wisdom to share. The good reverend showed up on and off in the books, but the show gave him meatier story lines.

MISS BEADLE: The first teacher we meet in prime-time Walnut Grove, the beloved Miss Beadle brought the love of education to the children, as well as the sweet smell of lemon verbena perfume.

MISS ELIZA JANE WILDER: The subsequent teacher, Miss Wilder (a.k.a. Manly's older sister), was stricter than Miss Beadle and probably smelled like sour pickles.

THE GARVEYS: Jonathan and Alice Garvey joined Walnut Grove midway through the show's run and immediately became BFFs with the Ingalls family. They shared the same work ethic, love of family, and high moral standards. Their son, Andy, was fast pals with Albert, and shenanigans ensued.

Home Sweet AF Home

CHAPTER 1
HACK YOUR FAMILY LIFE
BECAUSE PROBLEMS AREN'T ALWAYS SOLVED IN AN HOUR

HOME IS THE NICEST WORD THERE IS.
—LAURA INGALLS
SEASON 1 • EPISODE 1 • "A HARVEST OF FRIENDS"

I t's comforting to imagine that all families could be as happy and stable as the Ingalls family; they seemed to get along peachy as pie. Well . . . unless you noticed how mad Caroline became when Charles had to leave home yet again to find work and didn't check in with her to see how she was

1

feeling about it. Or how Laura and Mary frequently annoyed each other. Or how jealous Laura felt when Albert came to live with them and took Pa's attention away from her. *Or* how Albert got involved with the wrong crowd and returned home addicted to drugs. As with all families, there were a few pits in the peachy pie.

There were three marriages between the real Ingalls and Quiner families within a few years: Polly Ingalls married Henry Quiner in 1859, Charles Ingalls married Caroline Quiner in 1860, and Peter Ingalls married Eliza Quiner in 1861.

Just as ours do, families in Walnut Grove had their share of troubles. Some of them were unique to their time and place in history, but others came with lessons we all hope to learn: to accept one another, warts and all, to expand our ideas of what makes a family, to talk and *listen* to one another, to prioritize time together, to stay connected while living apart, and to try like hell to figure out parenting.

Let's just admit that we were slightly relieved to see even the happiest of *Little House* families deal with difficult circumstances in the books and on the TV show, just like we did. And like us, they didn't always handle things perfectly—even in the sugarcoated world of fiction. Still, we can learn a thing or two from our favorite frontier families.

Hack #1:
ACCEPT YOUR FAMILY FOR WHO THEY ARE

When Your Family Gets Your Goat

> **LAURA:** Mary, if I tell you something bad, will you tell Pa?
>
> **MARY:** Yes.
>
> **LAURA:** Oh. Good night, then. —*Season 3 • Episode 19 • "THE MUSIC BOX"*

Remember feeling the tension when Isaiah Edwards gave his son that shotgun, knowing full well that the only thing John Jr. wanted to shoot was the breeze? Isaiah assumed that because *he* loved hunting and farming, his son needed to as well. John Jr. was a prolific reader and writer, and we eventually learned that Isaiah couldn't read at all. His son was a constant reminder of this, and it made Isaiah feel ashamed. It took a darn bear to maul some sense into Isaiah, but luckily, he came around.

In another episode, Nels Oleson was mortified when his estranged sister showed up in town as the "Fat Lady" of the traveling circus. He'd always been ashamed of her, but after growing and maturing, he'd become more ashamed of himself and the way he was still treating her. Nels's embarrassment reflected his self-esteem, not hers. And until he realized his mistake, Nels was more worried about himself being the victim of bullying and teasing than his sister.

Victor French, the actor who portrayed the scruffy-but-lovable Isaiah Edwards, was a jokester right up until his death in 1989. No one was surprised when he left the humorous message "Eat Shit. Love, Victor" on a banner flying behind an airplane that flew over his funeral service.

Have you ever looked around your family table at Thanksgiving and thought, *Some of these people are seriously full of applesauce?* Everybody's got at least one relative (or three) with whom they don't connect. Next time, try this: Accept that your family members are who they are, and move on. Just let that sink in for a moment. Okay. You can breathe now and get on with your life.

If you're dreading a visit with a relative because disagreement is brewin' below the surface, hop on the phone ahead of time to discuss the tricky topic. If it feels extra tricky, send an email or text before the call to give them a heads-up. This proactive conversation may keep resentments from further accumulating and blowing up during your upcoming time together, which could also affect other family and friends during the visit.

It's tempting to wish you could create an entire family unit in which everyone thought, felt, and did things exactly as you do, but what fun would that be? How would you learn the valuable lessons of acceptance, patience, and communication?

How could you possibly be better prepared for future relationships that force you to deal with wildly differing political views, raised toilet seats, and excessively loud food-chewing?

Petty—and not-so-petty—annoyances are part of family life. The reality is, people can't live together day in and day out without getting on one another's nerves sometimes. And even those relatives we only see a few times a year can drive us batty.

> Remember when Almanzo's sister Eliza Jane came into town to help a very pregnant Laura after Manly's crippling stroke? Laura was irritated with the way she overly pampered her brother, ignoring Laura's wishes to take care of Almanzo herself. She might have accepted the help more willingly if Eliza Jane had encouraged him to become more independent, as Laura was trying to do. Still, Laura couldn't change the fact that her sister-in-law was family, even if she did drive her panta-loony; Eliza Jane only wanted to help. Ah, the trouble with in-laws. Sometimes you just have to bite your tongue and move on. (That, of course, doesn't mean you accept abusive or overly intrusive behavior. Boundaries aren't just for maps.)

If you dig deep, you eventually uncover the foundation of what causes most of your issues: expectations someone else should fulfill so that *we* feel more comfortable. This realization often brings up insecurities we'd rather not address. But if you acknowledge and accept this of yourself and receive others as they are, you can begin to let go of your angst and simply enjoy being around them.

When you expect someone to be just like you, you miss out on the incredible things you can learn from *their* unique qualities. Your family members may not always share your beliefs or values, but trying to change them would probably be as successful as them trying to change you.

Okay, maybe Laura needed to more quickly conclude that Fred the goat was *too* unique to become a permanent part of the Ingalls family. After all, he *did* have a terrible drinking problem and probably would have eaten Pa's work shirts.

Unpack the Hack

Think of a family member who gets under your skin. Write down the specific ways they do and any topics that spark arguments. Then make a list of subjects upon which you agree, even if they're as simple as building birdhouses or getting sucked into the latest crime drama. That list is hopefully longer than the cons, but even if it isn't, now you're armed with a selection of conversation starters that draw on your similarities. If the relative veers into argument territory at a family function, politely excuse yourself to talk to someone else—or go into the bathroom and scream into a hand towel.

Hack #2:
EXPAND YOUR IDEA OF FAMILY

Put Out the Welcome Mat

OH, MR. EDWARDS, THANK YOU, THANK YOU FOR GOING ALL
THE WAY TO INDEPENDENCE TO FIND SANTA CLAUS FOR US!
—LAURA INGALLS
LITTLE HOUSE ON THE PRAIRIE

Family doesn't have to be connected by DNA; in fact, we may
feel more kinship with blended or some non-blood relationships, thinking of them as "chosen family." Heck, with the
number of adoptions alone that took place in the fictional
Walnut Grove, the message was loud and clear: Families are
what we make them.

> To combat the problem of thousands of children living in the
> streets in the mid-1850s, orphans were placed on "orphan
> trains" and brought to towns where pioneer families were set-
> tling. Although Charles Loring Brace started the movement
> with good intentions, the children were often adopted only to
> serve as farmhands and experienced abuse. By the early 1900s,
> the Orphan Train Movement was over.

Family trees used to have multiple branches, and it
seemed like everyone had several siblings and at least a baker's

dozen of cousins. More recently, U.S. birth rates have declined. Adults are waiting much longer to have kids if they have them at all. As blood families become smaller, chosen ones expand with friends, coworkers, neighbors, and pets.

Charles and Caroline often complained that their tiny house was overcrowded with their growing family, so . . . they went ahead and adopted more kids. During its nine-season run, the show's revolving door of adoptions was admirable but almost comical.

+ The Ingalls family adopted Albert, rescuing him from a life as an artful dodger and all-around hooligan on the streets of Winoka.

+ James and Cassandra found refuge, a new last name, and regular servings of apple fritters with the Ingalls family after their parents died in a tragic covered-wagon rollover.

+ Jenny landed in Uncle Almanzo and Auntie Laura's home after her father, Royal (Manly's brother), met his maker.

+ John Jr., Alicia, and Carl's mother died after a struggle with cancer, leaving the children in the permanent care of flannel-clad Isaiah Edwards and his wife, Grace.

+ In season 9 (wait, there was a ninth season?), Isaiah flexed his fatherly muscles again and adopted young Matthew Rogers from the traveling snake-oil salesman's sideshow.

✦ Who could forget Nancy? The Olesons adopted this Nellie clone after the original grew up, got nice, and moved to New York with her husband and twins.

Most of us are born into our families, and like a Whitman's Sampler box, it's not necessarily filled with our favorite sweets. Sometimes a certain nut variety doesn't settle very well with us, or we wish we had a different selection. Why not choose your own? Friends can become so close that it only seems natural to make them a part of your family.

You could even say the Ingalls family more or less adopted Isaiah Edwards. Before moving to Walnut Grove, he was a troubled drifter who had lost his wife and daughter to a deadly illness. It wasn't long before he became more like a brother to Charles and a loving uncle to the children.

Sometimes art imitates life. Actors Melissa Gilbert (Laura Ingalls) and her real-life brother, Jonathan Gilbert (Willie Oleson), were both adopted. Brothers Patrick and Matthew Labyorteaux, who played Andrew Garvey and Albert Ingalls, were also adoptees.

As our world grows, so do our perceptions of what a family looks like. In pioneer days, most families (whether real or imagined) consisted of a ma and a pa, and if they were lucky, some surviving children. As people have come to feel more open about how they identify and whom they love, the look of a modern family has become as varied as that box of chocolates. Granted, a family with two moms or dads may have seemed strange to our favorite Plum Creek community back then, but we'd like to think the Ingalls family would have shrugged and set up another blanket next to them at the Sunday afternoon picnic. Everyone was welcome at their table.

When you lift the blinds and put out the welcome mat, you not only open your home to people who need love, you receive just as much from them. Pass the chocolates!

Unpack the Hack

Think about the friends and neighbors with whom you feel especially close, and invite them for coffee, a meal, or a fun outing. If it feels appropriate, let them know you feel like they're part of your family. This can create a meaningful connection, especially if the person is estranged from or doesn't have nearby blood relatives of their own.

Hack #3:
CREATE RITUALS AND CELEBRATIONS

Set the Family Table

SPECIAL DISHES AREN'T FOR SPECIAL TIMES,
THEY'RE FOR SPECIAL PEOPLE.
—CAROLINE INGALLS
SEASON 2 • EPISODE 19 • "FOR MY LADY"

On the prairie, family celebrations were as elaborate as their pocketbooks would allow. Nellie might have received yet another expensive French doll as a birthday gift, while the Ingalls girls would have been over the moon with a homemade dress or a fancy bonnet. Remember when each of the Ingalls girls was ecstatic over getting an orange in their Christmas stocking?

A fan-favorite episode was season 1's "Christmas at Plum Creek." Who wouldn't get the warm fuzzies watching family members work so hard to find one another the perfect gift for their first Christmas in their tiny house? Ma, clearly a saint, took the high road and let Mary claim the idea for Pa's gift, quickly hiding her identical hand-sewn shirt. Ma received a fancy seven-dollar stove, and the whole family was mesmerized by the simple tinfoil tree star that Carrie had managed to haggle Nels Oleson down on from five cents to a penny.

What was most wonderful wasn't the humble gifts or the crafty ways they came up with them; it was the obvious love and togetherness they shared. Especially after the long struggle they experienced building their new life, in the books and on the show, the Ingalls family knew that time spent together was the most perfect gift of all. (Cue the "awwws.")

Rituals and celebrations bring home the value of family and help you appreciate being a part of one. If you have kids, you know how difficult even a simple meal together can be. Busy after-school activities have families eating in the car while driving back and forth from practices and games. Making time for each other can be tough for young couples as well, with crazy work schedules, social commitments, and deadlines. But even during harvest season, the Ingalls family made time for some meals together. Pa may not have smelled daisy-fresh for every sit-down, but the family knew that his stink meant money, so they welcomed it.

> THAT WAS SUCH A HAPPY SUPPER THAT
> LAURA NEVER WANTED IT TO END.
> —LAURA INGALLS WILDER
> *THE LONG WINTER*

Spend the ritual of mealtime sitting down and turning off the TV, even if your favorite episode of *Little House* is on. This invites conversation and connection that are vital to family, couple, or even roommate bonding. At a minimum, put aside one sacred night a week on the calendar to do so—this togetherness effort can make all the difference. Whether you're concocting a six-course meal complete with homemade biscuits or you're ordering pizza, carving time out of your busy life to enjoy a meal together reminds everyone that family is a priority, and it helps you make lifelong memories. Don't forget to occasionally include friends and other special people that make up your "family." And remember not to overthink your home clutter and simple meal offerings. It's the togetherness that makes anything a five-star feast.

"Friendsgiving" was coined in 2007. It is celebrated around the U.S. Thanksgiving holiday and is used to celebrate gratitude and share meal festivities with friends. For some, it's an addendum to their Thanksgiving Day celebration with family. Others choose to make Friendsgiving their featured holiday and skip the family gathering.

Anyone visiting the Ingalls family's home for such a shindig most likely would have been treated to some of Caroline's apple fritters and most *definitely* would have boogied down to some of Charles's fiddle music.

That afternoon the finished black cashmere was carefully pressed, and then Ma made a big, white cake. Laura helped her by beating the egg whites on a platter with a fork until Ma said they were stiff enough.

"My arm is stiffer," Laura ruefully laughed, rubbing her aching right arm.

"This cake must be just right," Ma insisted. "If you can't have a wedding party, at least you shall have a wedding dinner at home, and a wedding cake."

—Laura Ingalls Wilder, *These Happy Golden Years*

Celebrations can recognize any milestones or wins, but it's just as important to break out the moonshine (or your beverage of choice) and gather round for no reason at all. But make sure none of your guests go missing; remember when Reverend Alden got married? Everyone gathered to celebrate, but then we never saw the lovely Mrs. Alden again. Another Walnut Grove mystery!

Take stock. You're probably already ritualizing parts of your life. Here are some common ones:

✦ Giving a kiss and an "I love you" as your partner leaves for work

✦ Calling your mom at the same time every day or week to check in

- ✦ Reading a book to your kids before they go to sleep
- ✦ Ordering takeout and watching a movie on Friday nights
- ✦ Having coffee with your partner and discussing the day ahead
- ✦ Stopping by a candy store as you begin a road trip (okay, maybe that one is just us)

Even small rituals can become traditions. In the "Ma's Holiday" episode, Charles took Caroline on an anniversary trip . . . without the kids! Fans probably hoped this would become an annual tradition, not only for romantic reasons but to get Ma the hell out of the kitchen for a spell. Do you and your family take an annual trip to a cottage or the beach? These kinds of rituals bond us as tightly as log walls in a cabin.

Let's take a cue from the Ingalls family and start making family connections a priority. Celebrate special times and remember that any time together is special. Making memories doesn't require making a fuss.

Unpack the Hack

Why save gatherings for the holidays? Adopt the idea of a fun-filled dinner party at any time to celebrate friends new and old. Add siblings and other relatives to the mix to create one big happy family (mixed nuts, anyone)? Like Caroline's special dishes, there doesn't have to be a special time to celebrate the loved ones in your life.

Hack #4:
PARENTING ON THE PRAIRIE

Corral the Kiddos

WELL, WHEN A MOTHER AND DAUGHTER HAVE BEEN
AS CLOSE AS WE HAVE, WE TEND TO NOTICE THINGS ABOUT
EACH OTHER THAT OTHER PEOPLE WOULDN'T.
—MA TO MARY
SEASON 7 • EPISODE 10 • "TO SEE THE LIGHT, PART I"

The *Little House* books reflected their strict nature of parenting: Children were to be seen and not heard. The prime-time Ingalls family addressed child-rearing challenges with a softer approach. Even so, they still had their share of eye rolls and back talk (hello, Half Pint), as that comes with any parenting territory, prairie or otherwise.

Whether or not you have children now (or see them in your future), you probably noticed a variety of parenting styles on *Little House*. Naturally, no one could match Caroline and Charles's parenting prowess, but even they took a wrong turn every once in a while. Remember Part 1 of "The Lord Is My

Shepherd" episode, when Ma gave birth to a baby boy? Even perfect Pa didn't notice how little Laura worried about being replaced by the son he had always wanted.

Jonathan and Alice Garvey gave Caroline and Charles a run for their money when it came to good parenting, but their family unit changed after Alice died in the fire at the school for the blind. Jonathan fell into a deep depression, began drinking heavily, and could no longer properly parent their son, Andy. Enter the Ingalls family, always ready to put out another chair at the table. They took on Andy's care until Jonathan could sober up and become emotionally ready to parent again. Jonathan showed us that parents aren't perfect; they're humans who sometimes face hard blows and difficult situations. If children see us fall and get back up, it shows them that even if things aren't handled perfectly, we can still prevail.

Don't you sometimes feel envious when you hear a child complain that they're bored? Boredom is a luxury, especially when we think about our pioneer ancestors. When nothing is scheduled, this invites us to use our imaginations and get creative. Don't be afraid to turn off electronic devices and tell your kids (or yourself) to find something to do!

Child-rearing is certainly easier when both parents are on the same wavelength. Nels and Harriet Oleson parented inconsistently and left their kids open to navigating their own young lives, or worse, playing their parents against each other. Nels told Willie not to eat candy before dinner, and before you knew it, Harriet was opening the jar and telling her son to help himself. Not only were their rules inconsistent, but they also weren't exactly the best role models individually. As a result, viewers all saw how those kids behaved. The tricky part of parenting is maintaining overall high standards but also understanding that each child responds according to their nature. Mary Ingalls was more of the rule-follower like her mother, and although kind and openhearted, she was a little more reserved with others. Like her pa, Laura couldn't hide her boisterous feelings even if she wanted to. She learned her lessons by making mistakes. No matter how unique their children were, Charles and Caroline held them to the same standards and loved them unconditionally.

> **LAURA:** Why can't you just be like the rest of the children and join in?
>
> **NELLIE:** My mother says we're not like the rest of the children.
>
> **LAURA:** I suppose she's right. —Season 2 • Episode II • "The Gift"

If we decide to become parents, it's only natural for many of us to hope for a child who will be a sports star, an artistic wonder, or a brainy whiz like we may have been. Other parents hope their kids will live the life they couldn't and excel in the things they wish they had access to as young people. Problems come when we *expect* our kids to enjoy something other than what they do, like Isaiah and John Jr. What you like to spend your time doing is a large part of who you are and your personality; allow your kids to have the same freedom.

Michael Landon practiced nepotism by casting three of his own children, the most notable being Leslie Landon, who played Miss Plum, the schoolteacher from season 9.

Kids are tuned in and can tell if their parents are disappointed in them. Parents' expectations can be so damaging, especially when it goes beyond whether a child chooses to play sports or take part in theater. If a child doesn't feel like they belong in their own household, that can lead to strained relationships and result in lifelong consequences for their mental health.

The Ingalls parents took the time to talk to their kids. Charles and Caroline didn't often respond with a dismissive "Because I said so." This automatic response to a child's many *whys* may seem the easier explanation, especially if the reason is complicated or a decision needs to be made in a hurry. Kids are curious, and these are teaching moments. Explain your reasons as best you can, or tell them you will discuss them later when there is more time. And if your chosen reply is just a feeling you get from years of experience? Tell them so. Kids understand more than you realize.

Parenting is hard work, whether you transport your kids in a station wagon or a covered wagon. With patience, consistency, and respect for the uniqueness of your children, you may just receive the Ingalls stamp of approval.

Unpack the Hack

Just about any parenting book will tell you that it's not a good idea to be a short-order cook for your kids. Do you think Ma would have stood by while Carrie refused to eat her beans and asked for rabbit stew instead? Naturally, you want your family to enjoy the meals you cook, and you can avoid making four versions of dinner and still give your kids a hand in choosing a meal. Allow each child to plan a meal regularly: weekly, monthly, whatever works for you. Even better, require that they assist in that meal's prep. Depending on their age, they could do anything from grabbing the lettuce from the crisper to chopping carrots.

Hack #5:
EVERYONE PLAYS A PART

Collectively Canning the Pickles

A prairie household couldn't be kept up unless everyone pitched in. You may complain about having to run to the store to pick up some butter, but would you rather sit your butt down on a stool and churn? The basic chores we take for granted were physical work back in the day: fetching fresh water, sweeping the day's mud and dirt from the floors, beating dirty clothes by the creek, scrubbing the outhouse. That kind of work makes our Swiffering laughable; however, our twenty-first-century homes run better when we divvy up the chore load.

In the pioneer days, kids would often start their day at first light by bringing in wood, boiling water, and tending to the farm animals. Around the age of nine or ten, boys and girls would start to work in the field. They also learned how to cook, make soap and candles, and sew. Meanwhile, we struggle to get kids to brush their teeth while we stagger to our electric coffeepot.

Taking care of household business wasn't only a responsibility of a pioneer parent. When they weren't in school, kids worked on the farm and chipped in with chores around the house and in the fields. These duties weren't simply a matter of being helpful; they were a matter of survival.

Modern lifestyles tend to allow children more freedom, but enlisting them to help with various chores gives them pride and ownership and allows them to become more independent. It may seem easier to let kids be kids and shirk a lot of responsibility, but their lives will only be more difficult when they are suddenly on their own and wondering how to cook and clean for themselves. Can you even imagine Willie Oleson's bachelor pad?

Allocating tasks is the best way to keep things running smoothly, especially when each person falls into responsibilities that feel natural to them. One person may feel more at home in the kitchen, so they take on most of the cooking duties. Others may enjoy outdoor work, so they care for the lawn and garden. Even young children can have their own chores like bringing the dinner plates to the sink, emptying their trash, or caring for a pet.

Being part of a family doesn't only require keeping up with our messy homes; you'll inevitably need to do your part to avoid or clean up some messy communication situations as well. If you're lucky, your family feels like a safe place where you can let down your pigtails and truly be yourself. Unfortunately, this can lead to communicating without filters in a brash or hurtful way, taking your frustrations out on one another.

It's easy to take bottled-up resentments out on our siblings, suddenly shouting, "I *know* it was *you* who burned fish sticks in my Easy Bake oven!" ten years after the damage was done. This can put your relationship in a serious pickle. The next time you want to lash out at a family member and say something you may regret, take a breath and think, *Would I say that to my best friend?* If something they said or did feels disrespectful, you have a right to feel angry . . . but talking it out calmly and respectfully (around the actual time of the incident would be best) will get better results and help you both feel more connected.

We suggest the challenge of holding yourself to the standards of the quintessential Ingalls parent (or at least as close as you can). As a mom or dad, sibling, or extended family member, see your familial relationships as things that need to be cared for and nurtured. Communicate with openness and love, clear a place at the table, and do the work to keep your relationships with kin and chosen family a priority. This is a constant work in progress, but when each member does their part, we have a much better chance of successfully canning those pickles.

Unpack the Hack

Recognize a family member for their contribution with a celebration plate! Buy one of the many available or designate one of your own. Don't save it only for special occasions; serve up dinner or dessert and set it in front of the guest of honor to applaud a job well done around the house or making the right choice with a difficult situation. Some plates come with a permanent marker to write each occasion on the back of the plate; this makes for great memories. If it doesn't come with a pen, use your own!

Pioneer Challenge:
A DILLY OF A SNACK
FOR THE FAMILY FRIDGE

Auntie Viv's Quickle Pickles

And speaking of pickles, who doesn't love a yummy sweet or spicy dill? One would think this is an arduous process, but this recipe won't bust your hump. We promise that these are pickles even Willie wouldn't want to get out of!

BRINE:

2 cups apple cider vinegar	2–3 tablespoons white sugar
2 cups white vinegar	5 tablespoons kosher salt
4 cups water	

PICKLING SPICE:

2 tablespoons whole black peppercorns	2 tablespoons dill seed or dried dill weed
2 tablespoons whole mustard seeds	1 tablespoon whole allspice berries
2 tablespoons coriander seeds	10–12 crumbled bay leaves (Don't skip! The tannins help preserve the crunchiness!)

Stir ingredients together in a small bowl. If you're short on time, we swear we won't tell Ma if you buy premade pickling spice.

OTHER INGREDIENTS:

4–5 pounds mini/pickling cucumbers

2–3 large cloves of garlic per jar, smashed

2–3 sprigs of fresh dill

4–6 (8-ounce) mason jars with lids

Want pickles as spicy as Nellie and Percival's kisses? Add 3–4 whole Thai chili peppers (split lengthwise, leaving the seeds inside—*wear gloves* and *do not touch your eyes or inside your pantaloons!*) and 5–6 jalapeños, sliced into rounds. Add 2–4 of these in each jar, depending on your spice preference. You can also add 1–2 teaspoons of crushed red pepper flakes.

INSTRUCTIONS:

Bring the apple cider vinegar, white vinegar, and water to a boil in a large pot. Add the sugar and salt, and then turn down to a simmer.

Meanwhile, assemble the cucumbers, garlic, dill, and any extra ingredients such as Thai chilis or jalapeños into the jars as desired. Pack them tightly, but not too much so! Add 2–3 tablespoons of the pickling spice mixture to each jar.

Pour the hot brine into each jar, covering the cucumbers and leaving about ½ inch of space under the lid. Give the jars a good shake to mix the ingredients well.

Tightly screw the lid and voilà! Quickle pickles! Bring these to your next Friendsgiving to wow your guests—they also make great holiday gifts!

PRO TIP: *Open the windows as you boil the brine. Boiling vinegar is smellier than Pa's boots on harvest day!*

CHAPTER 2

HACK YOUR COMMUNITY LIFE

DON'T UNDERESTIMATE THE POWER OF A GOOD POTLUCK

THERE IS NOTHING IN THE WORLD
SO GOOD AS GOOD NEIGHBORS.
—CAROLINE INGALLS
ON THE BANKS OF PLUM CREEK

I n Walnut Grove, you probably couldn't fart without the whole town getting wind of it, but in times of crisis or need, our favorite pioneer residents put differences aside and were there for one another. Thanks to the global pandemic, many of us have felt an increased desire to experience a sense of belonging and connection. One solution is to take a page from the Walnut Grove handbook! Get back to knowing your neighbors and getting involved in or creating your in-person and virtual communities.

The benefits of community connection are endless! It's useful to know people with pickup trucks when you need to move a love seat. It feels great to return the favor when a neighbor asks for help hanging outdoor holiday lights or tending to a pet. During tough times, it's nice to look to our community for job leads, doctor recommendations, lost dog searches, and even casseroles if someone's family is having a health crisis.

It's so easy now to find compatible communities online. Reverend Alden's mind would have been blown if he'd had that kind of reach. Can you imagine his Sunday service's live streams? Or a GoFundMe to rebuild the school for the blind after Albert accidentally burned it down while blazin' up the pipe tobacco in the basement?

Laura told her readers that good neighbors are what makes a neighborhood a community. Who are the people in *your* neighborhood, and how might you make those connections?

Hack #1:
SHARE THE LOAD AND THE WEALTH

It Takes a Township

In the pilot episode of *Little House on the Prairie*, the Ingalls family set out to make a new life outside the Big Woods. When they found a place to build a home, it didn't take long for Charles to realize he really could use some extra muscle. He set out to find a neighbor and came back with Isaiah Edwards. When the task was done, they went their separate ways, but Isaiah would later become Pa's lifelong friend and a key member of their community.

Being a part of a community means it's easier to find help when you need it, and it readily gives you opportunities to share. Most Walnut Grove residents were farming families, and one bad storm or grasshopper swarm might wipe out their annual income. In "The 100-Mile Walk" episode, the Ingalls family was mentally spending the future payout from their bountiful wheat haul when a nasty hailstorm turned their grateful OMG into a giant WTF. Pa soon joined the community of farmers on the long walk to help one another find work. And the whole time the menfolk were far away making moolah and trying not to die in dangerous quarry jobs, Ma organized the women and threw down some bonnet-busting work to save whatever they could from the damaged wheat crops.

Most people don't have to depend on their community to that degree, but you can certainly benefit from making local connections. From borrowing the stereotypical cup of sugar to lending a power washer, it feels good to know that your neighbors have your back.

"Borrowing a cup of sugar" is a phrase that was once used literally by neighbors who truly did need the sweet stuff but is now also a euphemism for being a nosy neighbor.

Community building is very much aligned with the historic barn-raising tradition. Both require enough people who are willing to come together to share their talents and strengths. With everyone doing their part, together they build something that wouldn't have happened if they were alone and create a sense of unity and belonging.

Historically, the practice of barn raising started with a farmer putting a call out for help to build a barn in one day. The framework for the structure was constructed carefully on its side and then lifted with the strength of many neighbors and livestock. Once all four walls and the roof frames were erected, the barn was "raised." Then it was time to celebrate with everyone, sharing food and drink and the pride of a job well done.

In prairie times, families depended on sharing resources when supplies were low. These days, with every product imaginable at the grocery store year-round, it's more of a convenience—though a worthy one! Think about opportunities to creatively share instead of buying new. Freecycle and similar sites, as well as social media "Buy Nothing" groups, have options for posting items you're willing to loan or give away to neighbors. A shared community garden plot is a fabulous way to split responsibilities and collectively reap the homegrown rewards. If you're zoned for raising chickens, become the "egg person" in your neighborhood. Trade fresh bread for handmade pickles (see Auntie Viv's Quickle Pickles recipe from the previous chapter). Carpool to the farmers' market on Saturday mornings . . . or even better, share the cost of your neighborhood booth at the market.

> While gardening, skip sitting in the dirt to measure the distance between plants. Instead, create soil-friendly glue by combining a cup of water and a tablespoon of cornstarch and stirring it constantly over medium heat until it thickens. Then, once cooled, use the "glue" as a base to adhere seeds to a pre-measured, biodegradable length of paper party streamer and plant them all at once, perfectly spaced.

Teaching kids the value of contribution is key to their becoming community-conscious adults. When Walnut Grove's church needed a new bell, the town's children donated some of their metal toys to melt for the cause. This was especially impressive given that these kids (minus the Oleson spawn) owned very few toys.

> Encourage the children in your life to contribute where they can. Maybe they save part of their allowance for a year and then donate it to their favorite nonprofit. Or they ask their birthday party guests to bring unwrapped toys, pet supplies, or nonperishable food items as a donation to the birthday child's organization of choice.

Extend one hand to repair a fence and another to pass along a loaf of banana bread. What you give with a happy heart tends to come back to you—that is, unless it's something you shouldn't be passing along; in which case, Doc Baker probably has something to treat it.

Unpack the Hack

Who doesn't have more than their share of stuff in their garages, closets, and cupboards? Perhaps it's time to recycle with a household item swap! This can be done with your physical neighbors, your friends, or an online group to which you belong. You never know—maybe somebody could use one of those old phone cases you've been hoarding.

With your close friends, you may want to meet up for cocktails and a clothing swap. Bring sweaters, shoes, skirts, coats, accessories, or anything that's been collecting dust in your closets and drawers. Throw everything in piles and take turns choosing by lottery, or with a fast and furious game of rock-paper-scissors. Whatever's left goes into a car, donation bound. Don't even think about bringing your leftovers back into your home, because they'll be gobbled up by the closet monster.

Hack #2:
OPEN YOUR ARMS AND YOUR HEART

Set an Extra Plate at the Table

HALF PINT, IF YOU DON'T STAND UP TO PEOPLE . . . BIGOTS . . . THEN YOU'RE NO BETTER THAN THEY ARE. WORSE, IN FACT, BECAUSE YOU KNOW THAT IT'S WRONG AND YOU ALLOW THEM TO THINK THAT YOU FEEL THE SAME WAY THEY DO.
—PA INGALLS
SEASON 5 • EPISODE 15 • "THE CRAFTSMAN"

For much of human history (and prehistory), our safety instinct told us to be afraid or distrustful of those we perceived as different from us. As time passed, we learned about the many ways those beliefs could lead to bigotry and discrimination. If you take the time to gain more understanding of others and the struggles they may have, you can better empathize with them. Empathy is a doorway to acceptance.

So let's address the elephant in the room. On the one hand, the *Little House on the Prairie* television series was a product of its less inclusive, narrower-minded times, especially toward Indigenous people and anyone of color. But the writers and producers did try to do better than the beloved book series, which was a product of its even *more* bigoted and narrower-minded times. While done in ways that induce some cringes today, in the 1970s and '80s, we saw a version of Pa who stood up for his Indigenous neighbors on multiple occasions, and provided shelter and love for Solomon, the young boy who'd run away to escape a future of enslavement. Ma and Pa Ingalls did their best to teach the girls that everyone deserves respect and friendliness, and to look beyond how someone dresses or the color of their skin. They advocated for many children during the show's nine-season run (wait, there were nine seasons?). Remember when young Spotted Eagle wanted to retain his Indigenous pride and refused to use the "white man's name" assigned by his light-skinned grandfather? Even though most of the town stood with their arms crossed instead of open, Pa and his family offered respect and a sense of belonging.

It's important to recognize that the '70s–'80s mindset was better than that of the Ingalls family's time, and our outlook today is better than that of the '70s–'80s. While so much of this can be painful, we can feel encouraged because it means we're all collectively learning and getting better. Efforts like those made by the TV series help steer us in the right direction.

Todd Bridges played Solomon in the "Wisdom of Solomon" episode. Just one year later, he began his most remembered role as Willis Jackson on *Diff'rent Strokes*.

Do you consider yourself a welcoming person? Granted, some of us are introverts and would rather wipe our butts with a dried corncob than hand-deliver a welcome basket to a new neighbor. But surely you could at least manage a friendly wave or nod in their general direction. When you're the new kid in the neighborhood or at work, any little gesture of welcome can mean a lot.

In rural farming communities, dried corncobs were often used as toilet tissue. They were sturdy, plentiful, efficient, and much softer on tender parts than you may imagine.

Unpack the Hack

Look beyond the typical welcome basket. If you notice a new neighbor has a pet, create something just for them. Include toys and treats, and write a "welcome to the neighborhood" card written by your own furry family member. If the pet's a cat, add some fresh catnip. If a pooch is a newcomer, include a list of the local dog parks (and poop bags—hint, hint!).

Alternately, if you spot a few houseplants in the windows, show up at their door with a smile and a "welcome plant."

> Along with their dog Jack (and Bandit, on the show), the Ingalls family had a couple of cats that weren't mentioned on the TV series. Black Susan lived with them in the Big Woods, and thank goodness for Kitty, mentioned in *Little Town on the Prairie*—she was such a good mouser, she stopped them from chewing off Pa's hair in the middle of the night!

Hack #3:
CREATE AND ATTEND EVENTS

Gather More Than Your Prairie Skirt

THAT'S THE BEST REASON
TO HAVE A PARTY . . . NO REASON AT ALL!
—PA INGALLS
SEASON 1 • EPISODE 7 • "TOWN PARTY–COUNTRY PARTY"

Then and now, the best "meet people in the community" bang for your buck is to host or show up at a gathering. You probably won't want to be known as the neighborhood wedding crasher or bris buster, so look for gatherings that make sense for you.

Save money and reuse! Create a community party box with plates, silverware, cups, candles, folding chairs, and more to pass among neighbors or friends so everyone doesn't have to buy new party supplies for each gathering. For ease, fill the box with neutral-colored items or choose the supplies with other group members.

Who doesn't love a good party? In pioneer days, just surviving the daily grind was probably reason enough to celebrate. Despite the homestead hustle, the townsfolk of Walnut Grove made time to celebrate together with picnics, church socials, Founder's Day celebrations, and even traveling carnivals. These were opportunities for neighbors to say howdy, mingle, join a pie-eating contest, or rope and ride a wild mule (we're looking at you, Charles and Nels).

Taking a work break and coming together to socialize and have fun helped the community get to know one another outside of a quick hello at the mercantile or organizing a rescue party to save kids from a runaway caboose.

During the Founder's Day festival in Walnut Grove, the aging logger "Bull of the Woods" challenged Pa in the logging competition. Pa could have easily won, but instead chose to let the Bull keep his pride. Good community members look out for one another and don't try to embarrass them when kindness is the better option.

> For parties, replace your ice with frozen berries, grapes, or citrus fruit wedges. Your guests' drinks will look festive and stay cold and refreshing.

Spending time with others you like is beneficial for your physical and mental well-being. When you feel more connected, you have lower rates of anxiety and depression and higher self-esteem, and you tend to feel more empathic toward others. No wonder Pa rarely suffered from anything more than milling-wheel injuries and farming mishaps. In general, Pa Ingalls was the heart of Walnut Grove, and connecting with others was his specialty.

> Maybe you'd rather take on something slightly low-key, so how about inviting a few people over for a game night combined with a wine tasting? Cover the wine bottle labels and have a blind taste test along with a vote. The winner gets a fancy bottle of vino to take home. We think Mr. Edwards would have been down with this idea, only he'd replace wine with moonshine. (Please note: We do not endorse this substitution.)

The prospect of entertaining neighbors in your home might feel intimidating. You've got the morning's dirty breakfast pans on the stove, and you *know* there's dog hair everywhere—what do you do? Anglican priest Jack King coined the modern term *scruffy hospitality*: deciding not to give a flying flapdoodle whether your house is picked up or there are dishes in your sink. It's perfectly normal and healthy to have pride in your home and want to show it off at its best, but if your high personal standards keep you from enjoying your house with others, you're missing out. After all, the people in a house are what makes it a home. Chances are if guests see some dishes on your counter, they're feeling relieved that they aren't the only ones who put off household chores. You can even make it easy on yourself and call for a potluck. Better yet, invite guests to bring musical instruments and call it a full-fledged hootenanny!

Originally known as *rummage sales,* garage or yard sales became a neighborhood event in the '50s and '60s. They were the result of increased advertising and affluence when people were accumulating more stuff than they could use.

Barbecues, holiday get-togethers, farmers' markets, garage sales, and block parties are just a sampling of the possible community smorgasbord options. Maybe your neighborhood garage sale results in selling your junk just to spend that money on someone else's, but remember that it's also another opportunity to check in on Marge's elderly pet iguana or ask how little Billy did at the science fair. And that woman down the street who bought the repeat deck of tarot cards you received as a gift? Suddenly you realize that she's into the woo-woo, just like you.

How lucky are you to have a variety of opportunities to keep connected and celebrate with one another? Just pick a day and drum up some togetherness.

Unpack the Hack

Invite your guests to create a collaborative playlist for your next party. On the invitation, ask them to drop their song choice(s) into your social media DMs, or text or email them to you. Be clear if you're looking for a specific theme or genre to match the party's tone. It might be a little jarring to hear Guns N' Roses at your intimate dinner party, but maybe that jangles your chain, so you do you. Caroline Ingalls swears by a fiddle-heavy playlist, but she's sleeping with the band.

Start a gourmet dinner club! Even if "gourmet" turns into an excuse to drink Two Buck Chuck (Charles's favorite wine) and laugh together, this is a great way to make a regular date night with your friends and neighbors. Have the hosts plan the meal and assign each person a dish . . . or wing it (literally!) by ordering in pizza and wings and call it good.

Take a cue from the *Little House* schoolhouse and let the kids in the neighborhood create a play. On performance day, everyone can get together and enjoy the creativity and fun. Collect cash or nonperishable items and donate them to a charity drive for your local shelter.

Hack #4:
STAY SAFE

Circle the Wagons

HERE, PA SAID, HE'D HARVESTED A CROP
HE DIDN'T KNOW HE HAD PLANTED. A HARVEST OF FRIENDS!
—LAURA INGALLS
SEASON I • EPISODE I • "A HARVEST OF FRIENDS"

When Charles injured his back in the very first episode, he was fortunate to have his new neighbors help with his work deadline at the mill—the Ingalls family would have lost their home if the work hadn't been finished on time. It's great to have the support of a community when the skies are blue, but we're particularly grateful for it when the storm clouds roll in. You may not have to sign up for a meal rotation when a neighbor's child falls into a mine shaft, but when someone's family member is in the ER with a fractured tibia, you might hop over to feed their dog.

IF WE STAND TOGETHER, YOU DON'T HAVE TO BE AFRAID.
—MARY INGALLS
SEASON 3 • EPISODE 9 • "THE BULLY BOYS"

Even the best planners among us can't predict some of life's misfortunes, and online communities expand the idea of "neighbors." You've probably seen your share of crowdfunding efforts on social media for causes like medical procedures, replacing clothing after a house fire, or helping pay a pet's expensive surgery bill. Many friends and neighbors are willing to step up if they can when tragedy strikes. Even if you don't have the financial means to assist, you can reach out and help in other ways: Childcare, meals, rides, errands, collecting mail, and housework are just a few ideas. When struck by a personal catastrophe, some don't even know what they need. Don't hesitate to offer suggestions, or simply *do* the helping. Sometimes the best thing you can do for someone who is grieving or overwhelmed is to take the lead, so they don't have to.

> Fill a resealable bag with various personal items, such as socks, hats, hand warmers, granola bars, bottles of water, and toothbrushes. Keep them in your car to share with people asking for assistance. You might even want to link up with other folks in coordinating to provide these kinds of items to people in your community who need them.

The fine folks of Walnut Grove were always ready to assist when someone needed a helping hand. When cancer took Mrs. Sanderson's life, Isaiah and Grace Edwards took in John Jr., Carl, and Alicia. No one could predict the Coopers' freak wagon incident that orphaned James and Cassandra. The Ingalls family gave them safe shelter and eventually adopted them. This was *after* they'd adopted that rapscallion, Albert. Charles and Caroline were the go-to people to assist when tragedy struck, especially in the "adopting orphans" category.

> The newly orphaned James Cooper was Jason Bateman's first acting role. Since then, he's amassed an impressive acting and directing career.

While no one can predict when and how they'll suddenly need help, it's good to have a plan in case you find yourself in the middle of an emergency. Know which friends and neighbors would be willing to quickly step in and help if you were stuck in a hospital, dealing with a burst pipe in your home while vacationing in Mexico, or needing to borrow a generator during a power outage. Have an "in case of emergency" list of your neighbors' phone numbers, and make sure they have yours. After all, no one can plan for a ladder fall while holiday decorating . . . or a growling pack of prairie wolves surrounding their home in the middle of the night.

> When smarty-pants Mary couldn't afford to go to a special math competition in Minneapolis, the townspeople came together and donated what they could so she could participate. Poor Mary felt the pressure to do well and not let her community down, but they assured her that she made them proud just by being there to represent their town.

Times of need don't always come from crisis. Loving encouragement can be shown in so many ways for so many reasons. Keeping up on what's happening in your neighbors' lives creates giving and receiving opportunities like meals for a new baby's arrival, or other causes for celebration. How about shoveling a sidewalk or raking a yard for an elderly person or for someone who is out of town? Or supporting the neighborhood kids with their school and scouting fundraisers? Who doesn't love being solicited with boxes of Tagalongs?

Unpack the Hack

Create a neighborhood group on social media. This can be a useful spot to ask for and provide help to your community. It can also be a place for drama to live, so pick an admin who's not afraid to click the Delete button. Caroline Ingalls would never put up with such nonsense.

If you haven't already, take a CPR course (or any other emergency intervention) and let your neighbors, coworkers, and friends know you're certified. Or make the class a community event for all to learn together.

Collect extra cans of food and other supplies to share in case there's a weather emergency and a friend or neighbor hasn't prepared. Post about your surplus on your neighborhood's social media group.

Combine safety with your Welcome Wagon. When a new neighbor moves in, bring a copy of the neighborhood contact list right over with goodies and an introduction. Make sure to have consent before sharing anyone's contact info.

Hack #5:
NOSY NEIGHBORS AND THE GOSSIP MILL

Don't Encourage the Negative Nellies

LOVE EACH OTHER. CARE ABOUT EACH OTHER. FORGIVE EACH OTHER'S MISTAKES, AND WE'LL ALL BE BOUND CLOSER TOGETHER . . . IT'S THE GIFT OF LOVE THAT'S THE GREATEST GIFT OF ALL.
—REVEREND ALDEN
SEASON 2 • EPISODE II • "THE GIFT"

Gossip *has* always and *will* always exist. In online and IRL communities, some people thrive on creating drama and feeding it into the gossip mill. Harriet Oleson took gossip-mongering to the next level. For a short time, she even wrote a Harriet's Happenings column in the *Pen and the Plow* newspaper. In that episode, Nels reminded his wife that a reporter's job is to be accurate, but Mrs. Olesen suggested she's merely "reporting the fact that they are rumors."

I LOOK FOR THE HUMOR OF MRS. OLESON. SHE WAS
ORIGINALLY PAINTED AS JUST BLACK-AND-WHITE MEAN.
ANYONE THAT MEAN HAS TO BE A FOOL. SO I BEGAN
MIXING FARCE INTO IT. I THINK THE AUDIENCE COUNTS
ON SEEING MRS. OLESON FALL ON HER FANNY
AND GET HER COMEUPPANCE.
—KATHERINE MACGREGOR
ON PLAYING HARRIET OLESON

People who seem to thrive on drama typically have a long history of failed relationships. Because of the way they tend to see the world, nosy or disapproving neighbors more than likely take everything you do personally, even if it doesn't affect them at all. Sadly, these people just end up pushing others away, which is in direct contrast to what the injured person probably wants most of all: connection and acceptance.

Rumors and gossip can isolate people in their neighborhoods and social communities. When someone is aware that they are the subject of gossip, it can affect their focus and even cause them to avoid going to school or work. Perhaps you'll feel like a Mary Ingalls goody-goody, but you can stop gossip in its tracks if it makes its way to you. Ask yourself how you'd feel if someone were spreading personal information about you, and be direct with the spreader. Tell them you're not interested in what they have to say.

In the sixth season of your favorite show on the prairie, you got a glimpse into what could very well have been contributing to Harriet's behavior. It turns out that she was engaged before she met Nels, and her fiancé broke it off, breaking her heart in the process. This more than likely left her feeling abandoned, invisible, and a bit out of control of her life. As a result, she was going to make sure she could not be ignored and that she was a part of everything and anything around her, whether she was invited or not!

And if you find the gossip is aimed toward you? Remember, a hurtful person is a hurting person; let this become your mantra. When you remind yourself of this, good ol' empathy comes to the rescue of your sanity once again. Happy people generally don't act like such a pain in the carbuncle.

If you find out your neighbor has been asked for a divorce or lost their job, choose kindness. Depending on how close you are to the person, you may stop by and have a conversation, or you may simply offer a smile and a wave if you see them in their yard. Any sign that lets them know you care and aren't a part of the negative gossip machine is supportive.

Unpack the Hack

Spread something positive about someone. If your neighbor just baked the best carrot cake you've ever tasted, tell your mutual friend. If a social media friend wrote a book, share a link (hint, hint). If your coworker created a kick-ass organizational system, bring it up to your pals over lunch. When we choose to use our powers for good, we boost spirits and send sparkly vibes out into the world. So tell your inner Mrs. Oleson to suck a pickled egg and opt for kindness.

When you are faced with neighbors who burn your biscuits even after you've tried your best to get along, embrace a little bit of feng shui magic. Place a mirror on your door to reflect bad energy outward. (You can even face it toward the culprit if they live to the left or right of you.) Wind chimes, yard decorations, or even flowers can help dispel the negativity. Is this really magic? Probably not. But it brings positive, intentional energy into your home, which is never a bad thing!

We hope this chapter will inspire you to not only ask, "Won't you be my neighbor?" to those around your literal and virtual neck of the woods but also pull up your sleeves and get ready to help raise that barn, share the wealth, and leave the gossip at the mercantile. Join National Night Out opportunities and the ubiquitous book clubs, get creative with progressive dinners, and don't forget rousing game nights, where you can really get to know your neighbors over a game of Cards Against Humanity.

Pioneer Challenge:
THRIFTY COMMUNITY COSTUME PARTY

Don't save dress-up fun for Halloween. Get your neighbors together by hosting a neighborhood theme party and request your guests come dressed accordingly. One catch: You must resourcefully create your costume using your existing wardrobe or something thrifted or borrowed. Here are some fun ideas for themes:

+ *Little House on the Prairie* (duh!)
+ Rock and roll
+ Superhero
+ Pun or wordplay-related (think: a formal apology, smart cookie, or party animal)
+ Your favorite food
+ True-crime characters

CHAPTER 3
HACK YOUR FAITH

WHATEVER THAT LOOKS LIKE TO YOU

LAURA FELT A WARMTH INSIDE HER. IT WAS VERY SMALL,
BUT IT WAS STRONG. IT WAS STEADY, LIKE A TINY LIGHT
IN THE DARK, AND IT BURNED VERY LOW BUT NO WINDS COULD
MAKE IT FLICKER BECAUSE IT WOULD NOT GIVE UP.
—LAURA INGALLS WILDER
THE LONG WINTER

aith can be much more than spiritual belief; it's part of your everyday life and can manifest itself in many ways. As well as a strong belief in a specific religious doctrine, faith is also defined as "complete trust or confidence in someone or something," according to the *Oxford English Dictionary*. You regularly call upon (and test) your faith in the people and world around you. Whom do you trust to relay global and local news to you? Can you have faith in the world as a whole and the goodness of your fellow human beings? You may not always have answers, but you can have faith. However you choose to practice faith, its purpose is to bring you peace.

Although the original congregational church in Walnut Grove was demolished decades ago, the church's bell now hangs in the belfry of the town's English Lutheran church and is rung every Sunday morning.

For those who grew up watching the show, you sat in Reverend Alden's tiny church from the comfort of your home, and his sermons never shied away from teaching traditional Christian values. But if you read between the quoted lines of scripture, you'll find that the heart of his message wasn't so much about any specific denomination or belief but was a general message of faith.

Faith makes you vulnerable (in the best way) and gives you hope. Pioneers like the Ingalls family depended on it daily because their lives were rife with uncertainties. They wouldn't have gotten far without their faith—faith in a greater power, themselves, one another, their friends, their community—and the belief that with faith, they could handle whatever came their way. Not even Pa knew if each day might bring a sweet side gig making wagon wheels . . . or the possibility of a rabid raccoon (Jasper!) running amok in his barn.

Although Michael Landon, *Little House*'s executive producer, writer, and star, centered the show around the Ingalls family's Christian values, the actor himself was Jewish.

Even with modern conveniences and the ever-growing information highway at your disposal, you are endlessly called to put faith and trust in yourself and one another as you forge your path. How can you discover and use *your* brand of faith to motivate you to be your best self and find peace? Thankfully, your favorite Walnut Grove family and friends left us a road map. The map may have streaks of Ma's fresh-churned butter on it, but you can read it just fine.

Addressing the topic of faith can be as awkward and sensitive as Miss Eliza Jane Wilder on a first date. Though we authors aren't conventionally religious, there is much to admire in the Ingalls family's love for God and the way it informed their lives' faith. It was such an important part of the books, the television show, and in pioneer times and is equally essential in your own life today. So climb up and take the faith cart out for a *Life Hacks* spin.

Hack #1:
FIND AND OWN YOUR FAITH

Write Your Recipe

There's no one right way to practice faith. You find comfort in what works for you and, like a recipe that's been passed down for generations, it can change over time. You may love Grandma's Sufferin' Succotash just the way it is. Or, with time, you could realize that the lima beans just don't sit well with you anymore. You may decide to substitute a different bean or leave them out altogether.

> **LAURA:** I don't think Mr. Pike has faith. He doesn't go to church.
> **PA:** It doesn't necessarily mean he doesn't have faith. He could be praying his own way, same as we did out on the prairie.
> —Season 2 • Episode 5 • "Haunted House"

Although your beliefs, practices, and bean preferences may vary, faith is typically based on the same universal principles of love, acceptance, reverence, trust, and forgiveness. Some of you grew up like most of the Walnut Grove kids: sitting in pews, listening to a leader share lessons and parables. Some of you still sit in places of worship and find meaning in God or a higher power every day. Others find fellowship in drum circles, on prayer mats, or through nature-based rituals. Walking meditations in the woods provide all the inspiration some need to clear their mind, feel peace, and have faith in the goodness of people. Still others look within as their source of faith, believing their choices alone determine their destiny.

> The Reverend Edwin Hyde "Robert" Alden was one of the real people on which Laura Ingalls Wilder based a character in the book series, and his character also appeared in the TV series.

While navigating faith's place in your own life, you may find yourself feeling pressured to adopt someone else's system of beliefs simply because you grew up with it, or it's what people around you lean on. Caroline made sure Charles parked his butt in a Sunday pew, but he also often found his church in the fields. Find your version of the "Pa standing in the sun-kissed crops" sanctuary, whether it be in an actual house of worship or another area of vocation. If you're not sure what that is, you may try finding guidance in books, prayer, meditation, journaling, or visiting a study group or holy place. Remember, if one prescribed set of beliefs and practices isn't for you, your faith can be more of a stew: a blend of various ingredients that create your brand of warmth and comfort.

> On the television show when the Ingalls family sat down to a nice hot bowl of Ma's home-cooked stew, they were actually eating Hormel's Dinty Moore from the can. Dinty Moore wasn't a person, by the way. The name was taken from a character in a 1913 cartoon by George McManus called *Bringing Up Father*.

Whether you're a believer in something bigger than your-self or the power of free will (or a stew of the two), *you* do *you*.

Unpack the Hack

Grab a journal or notebook and write about what comes to mind when you think of the word *faith*. What does it bring up? Do you feel pain or trauma? Peace or contentment? As you empty your thoughts and feelings onto the paper, pay atten-tion to them and ask yourself if you're fulfilled or if you may want to explore other facets of faith. Educate yourself about different faiths, and keep an open mind to what others' prac-tices can show you. And remember, there's no wrong answer when it comes to your relationship with faith.

Hack #2:
HAVE FAITH IN YOURSELF

Always Go for the Blue Ribbon

Mary's husband, Adam Kendall, had been blind most of his life, yet after (another) freak blasting oil explosion, he miracu-lously regained his sight and no longer felt satisfied teaching at the school for the blind. Talk about mind-blowing! Unsure of the outcome, he took the exam to become an attorney. Spoiler alert: He passed the exam, but there were hella setbacks along the way. Faith in yourself doesn't stop being necessary after you've taken that first step; persistence, even when things feel as bleak as poor Adam getting robbed in a rainy train station, is part of the journey.

> McCray and Co. is the fictional company that supplied the blasting oil that explodes and results in Adam's injuries. It was named for Kent McCray, one of the show's producers, as well as Landon's close friend and business partner. Was there some hidden message there? We're not sure, but this "tribute" didn't stop McCray from producing 'til the end of the show's run.

One of the most powerful ways to experience faith is simply by having faith in yourself. Gathering the confidence to explore new hobbies, apply for jobs, or ask out that cutie from the coffee shop doesn't always come easily, but most of us would rather risk feeling a little uncomfortable than miss out on these life-fulfilling possibilities.

DON'T BE AFRAID TO FAIL. BECAUSE IF YOU'RE NOT AFRAID AND YOU FAIL, IT DOESN'T MAKE YOU WEAKER, IT JUST MAKES YOU STRONGER.
—LAURA COLBY INGALLS
TO YOUNG CHARLES

Past victories or mistakes can affect your confidence. If you've baked the tastiest corn bread ever, you might have more faith in yourself going for a blue ribbon at the county fair. If your family politely smiles and asks if corn bread is something that could be added to a compost bin, you may feel further away from that ribbon. We must untangle our self-worth and faith in ourselves from being so directly connected to win/lose.

> In most cases, bread and baked goods shouldn't be added to a compost pile because they can attract pests; however, you can avoid this problem by using a compost bin with a tight-fitting lid.

One of our biggest fears is failure, and it can be paralyzing. Failure may be a "lack of success," but then, how do you define *success*? Try redefining it. You may not accomplish something in the way that you'd planned, but as you go through the painstaking process, you learn and grow. When the Walnut Grove community raised money for math whiz Mary to attend a prestigious competition and she didn't finish in first place, she returned to the town feeling like she'd let everyone down. However, she soon learned that they were still proud of her, and her participation and representation of Walnut Grove was a win. It's easy to write something off as defeat, but these bumps only make you more resilient and better prepared for what's down the trail. Those so-called failures become lessons. And your "wins" inspire natural confidence so you're ahead of the game the next time around.

> Your posture can make a big difference in your self-confidence. Sit up straight, let your shoulders drop, and flatten your lower back . . . instant confidence boost!

It's time to redefine *success* and *failure*. Listen, if Nellie Oleson could eventually make an edible plate of ham and eggs, you can write a kick-ass résumé or finish a first draft of that novel. Have a little faith in yourself!

Unpack the Hack

Change your passwords to compliments or affirmations. When logging onto your favorite shopping site, wouldn't you rather have to type BLUERIBBONCORNBREAD#1 than FLUFFY123? Every little thing counts when it comes to increasing your confidence and courage.

Hack #3:
FIND FAITH IN OTHERS AROUND YOU

Open Your Arms

THINGS AND PERSONS APPEAR TO US ACCORDING TO THE LIGHT
WE THROW UPON THEM FROM OUR MINDS.
—LAURA INGALLS WILDER
FARM JOURNALIST: WRITINGS FROM THE OZARKS

Where would you be without faith in your fellow human beings? Remember how Caroline gave Isaiah the hairy eyeball the first time she saw him? She was quick to judge his rough-and-tumble exterior and was soon proven wrong as he consistently came through with kind support for her family.

....

THERE'S GOOD IN ALL PEOPLE.
IT'S A LITTLE BIT HARDER TO FIND IN SOME.
—REVEREND ALDEN
SEASON 2 • EPISODE I • "THE RICHEST MAN IN WALNUT GROVE"

....

It's easy to jump to conclusions and distrust others, especially if you've been burned in the past. And if you've fallen down the rabbit hole of negative social media comments, you may find yourself thinking the worst of everyone. Even Laura's beloved pooch Jack couldn't find his way out of one of *those* dogpiles.

Given the choice, most people will choose kindness and goodness. Quick test: What would you do if you found a wallet on the street? You'd probably do your best to try to find the owner because that's what Charles would do. Now think about your circle of friends. Most if not all of them would do the same, right? Now look at the people in your town and your community, and trust that it's likely what most of them would do as well.

In late 1800s prairie life, pioneers didn't have access to 24-7, in-your-face news channels. Letters might take weeks to arrive, and people were lucky if they were able to get outside information from limited newspaper printings or a traveling merchant's word of mouth. That's a little different from an immediate iPhone notification informing you about a current event happening on the other side of the world.

On the other hand, handsome Caleb Hodgekiss (played by the one and only Johnny Cash!) came rolling into town, and everyone was quick to believe that he was indeed a preacher, collecting money for the poor instead of filling his own pockets. **LESSON**: Trusting everyone is going to throw you into a ring of fire sometimes, but it's still a good mindset.

With news and opinions coming from all directions these days, it helps to remember that much of what you see in the media is skewed. Fear marketing and clickbait headlines are a thing. When you're afraid, you are more likely to keep tuning in to the channel that's reporting the latest catastrophe or buying whatever is being sold under the guise of safety. Humans experience "loss aversion": the psychological principle that we are more responsive and motivated by the fear of loss than the hope of attaining something.

We feel afraid when we're not in control. This is why any form of faith can be difficult; we are called to relinquish some of that control. You may not have power over what other people say or do or what happens in the world around you; however, you do have the choice of whom you get involved with and what you expose yourself to. Although the media grows and keeps its audience by having us believe the entire world is in chaos at all times, the uplifting (and unprofitable) news is that there really is more good than bad in the world.

The 1932 Serenity Prayer that has been reworded and adopted by twelve-step programs everywhere reminds us to accept the things we cannot change, have the courage to change the things we can, and embody the wisdom to know the difference. Whether you view this sentiment as a prayer or simply wise words to live by, use them to remind you to focus on the good of the world, surround yourself with community, and do what is in your power to foster peace when and where you can.

And when you feel yourself slipping into doom and gloom, instead of complaining about how bad a situation is—especially those out of your control—find ways to get involved in a cause you're passionate about. You can do this alone or with kindred spirits. Organize a volunteer group to pick up trash in the park or make sandwiches for shelters.

If you're planning a community cleanup day, funds don't necessarily have to come out of your own pockets. Make a list of your needs, along with prices, and ask for donated money or supplies from local businesses.

Now of course Walnut Grove residents weren't as bombarded with global negative news as we are, but they still had the Harriet's Happenings gossip column to rile everyone and pit neighbor against neighbor. There is always a Harriet, isn't there?

When telephone service came to Walnut Grove, Harriet Oleson agreed to be the switchboard operator. No one realized until it was too late that gossip girl Harriet stayed on the line and listened to everyone's phone calls. Laura and Albert decided to teach her a lesson by setting up a call sharing a phony stock tip. Harriet acted on the tip and lost a pile of their family's savings. This was one of the many reasons why no one had faith in Harriet Oleson to keep tight-lipped about personal information . . . or most anything.

But thankfully, most of us don't have multiple Harriet Olesons in our lives. Give people the benefit of the doubt and remember that a bad experience with one person doesn't mean it'll be the same with everyone.

Unpack the Hack

Give yourself a break from in-your-face news. Stop the notifications on your devices. Extra credit: Begin following social media pages that feature positive news, wholesome stories, and photos or videos of things like chickens riding on the backs of goats. Check in with yourself throughout the day about your ratio of good news versus bad news. Do you now want to adopt a goat and name him Almanzo? Good.

Hack #4:
BE STRONG AND HAVE COURAGE

Tighten Those Suspenders

Strength got the pioneers through many challenges, and they relied on the combined strength of family and neighbors. Pa often had to pull himself up by his bootstraps to endure yet another damaged crop. These days, if food goes bad, hopefully you only need the strength to drive to the grocery store—or place an order for delivery. But moving through the death of a loved one, a medical crisis, loss of income, or any number of situations that drop you to your knees requires immense strength. Heck, getting through the day without taking a swipe at an annoying coworker sometimes takes all the strength we can muster.

Keeping faith requires a healthy mix of strength and courage. At first, those words seem similar, but when you picture yourself in a situation that requires one or the other, you'll find that they are quite different. It takes strength to endure something difficult and the vulnerability of courage to act bravely without knowing the outcome.

+ It took **STRENGTH** for the Ingalls family to survive
  travel across the plains with only what they could carry.
  It took **COURAGE** for them to leave their little house in
  the Big Woods to voyage into the unknown, in hope
  of a better life.

+ Ma and Pa had the **STRENGTH** to stick to their beliefs to shelter and protect an Osage chief in their home and the **COURAGE** to stand up to the local law enforcement.

+ It took **STRENGTH** for young Albert to survive on the streets of Winoka. It took **COURAGE** for him to trust the Ingalls family and accept their help.

Think about the times you demonstrated courage. Asking for a raise? Being honest about your feelings with a partner? Attending your first therapy session? Courage can come in small ways. Even attempting a new recipe for a dinner party could require some courage, although we recommend you try the recipe first. Oh, and don't let Laura near it with a container of cayenne pepper.

Who could forget the episode in which Nellie, trying to win the heart of Almanzo, prepared his favorite dish of cinnamon chicken? In an act of jealousy and spice sabotage, Laura replaced the cinnamon with cayenne and poor Manly paid the price.

How do you gather the strength or the courage you need when it's required? Can you imagine how Jonathan Garvey felt when he lost his wife in a fire? The same fire that took the life of Adam and Mary's infant son? It took a lot of strength to get through that kind of loss, and courage to ask for help to move forward in their grief.

And we've got to give a shout-out to poor, henpecked Nels. It took a massive amount of strength for him to put up with

Harriet every damn day, and a bushelful of courage to stand up to her. She was a force to be reckoned with!

Finding your strength and your courage go hand in hand with strengthening your faith. Having trust that you can eventually move forward and take the steps to do so requires both. When you can keep yourself from getting stuck in victim mode and carry on without blame, you enter a refreshing new territory of life that feels more and more like your true destination.

Unpack the Hack

Read books and watch movies about people who are courageous in the way you'd like to be. It's easier to find confidence when you're inspired by someone who's been there.

Hack #5:
FIND COMFORT IN FAITH

Embrace Space and Grace

When you experience loss or pain of any kind, it can be hard to imagine how life could ever be anything beyond torturous.

Comfort doesn't look the same to everyone, and what you need in one situation may look different in another. Once you get to a place where you can quiet that nasty lizard brain's voice for a bit, remind yourself that everything is cyclical. This level of sadness will ebb and flow, and even one day can make a difference.

After young James was shot in a bank robbery, slipped into a coma, and was sure to die, Pa was overcome with grief and anger. Although his family tried to comfort him, he couldn't make sense of such a situation. He left home with James in his arms and went into the mountains, where he built an altar and begged God not to take James. (PS: This is the only episode that features Pa with a beard. Good news for those of you who had "Pa sports facial hair" on your *Little House* bingo card.)

Hope can be found in a new day, as tomorrow is always filled with possibilities. Don't make light out of any challenges you may be going through; you can't just shut those feelings off, nor should you. Even if you awake to find your situation hasn't changed, you may receive a kind gesture or find a new source of comfort. You may even experience some kind of revelation, like maybe it's time you put on some *actual pants*, and that might be enough to turn things around for at least a moment.

For some, prayer is a huge part of finding comfort. Others would rather spend time in nature, cuddle their pet, or sit with a good friend and cry over cups of tea (or wine). If you're the one providing comfort, remember that you're not there to fix anything. Just lending your ear and sharing your heart can replenish someone in pain and give them some much-needed peace and the space to feel what they're feeling.

Despite what others may say, try to believe things don't happen for a reason; they happen for an opportunity. You can have faith knowing that someone who has passed on is at peace, and something that's lost clears the path for something new. You can trust that mistakes lead to wisdom gained and a chance to do it better the next time around.

"Remember me with smiles and laughter, for that's how I will remember you all. If you can only remember me with tears, then don't remember me at all" was a poem read by Reverend Alden at Julia Sanderson's funeral ("Remember Me, Part 1," season 2, episode 7). Melissa Gilbert included this poem in her social media tribute to him on the thirtieth anniversary of his death.

It's important to feel your entire range of feelings. The timing of the journey looks different for everyone. Think about how far you've come after a period in which you felt your world was collapsing. Give yourself space and grace.

Unpack the Hack

Toxic positivity is invalidating someone's painful emotions by suggesting they keep a positive mindset. Even with good intentions, forcing positivity on another can hurt more than help. Do your part to remove toxic positivity from your relationships, both on social media and in person. Remember that some social media friends and influencers use their "life is perfect" filter, even though they may be going through something painful behind the scenes. Don't compare your everyday life to someone else's highlight reel.

Here are some suggestions to replace the "just stay positive" advice you may feel compelled to offer a struggling friend:

+ That sounds really hard.
+ I'm here if you need to talk. Or not talk.
+ There's no set timetable for grieving.
+ Take all the time and space you need.

Pioneer Challenge:
"ALTAR" YOUR PERCEPTION

An altar most typically calls to mind a church or spiritual practice, but it can simply be any surface or space that invites you to take a much-needed pause and connect with peaceful feelings. Create a simple altar with any intentional objects or mementos that you hold sacred and that represent something special. It could be objects you place around a frame or a mirror, or an entry table filled with cherished photos. Use it for whatever reason feels right to you; there are no rules. Pray, meditate, touch the items, and take in the warm feelings. They can even hide in plain sight on your kitchen counter or living room bookcase! Simply walking by an altar every day can help you connect with some much-needed peace of mind.

CHAPTER 4

HACK YOUR ROMANTIC LIFE

LOVE, AMERICANA-STYLE

**LIFE SURE WAS A LOT EASIER
WHEN WE DIDN'T LIKE BOYS.**
—LAURA INGALLS
SEASON 2 • EPISODE 13 • "THE TALKING MACHINE"

I n pioneer days, "getting hitched" was mostly a practical endeavor. Many marriages were arranged, and these unions ensured the sharing of household chores and duties. Thankfully, choosing a romantic partner has evolved into more of a matter of the heart, but either way, relationships are hard work. Ma and Pa Ingalls weren't the envy of every couple on the prairie by happenstance; they made their relationship a priority through healthy communication, teamwork, and a little creativity.

Romantic partnerships can fall into a rut when the partners don't prioritize each other, leading to crankiness, unhealthy communication habits, lack of intimacy, and plain old boredom. Like the ruts left by the many pioneer wagons heading west, a long-term union leaves a lasting impression. With your eyes on the horizon and your intentions to guide you, the trail you take is more likely to be smooth and well-worn rather than rocky and tough to navigate.

The ruts made over two hundred years ago from the wagons of the Oregon Trail can still be seen today in Guernsey, Wyoming.

Many episodes of *Little House on the Prairie* depict their share of sweet (and sometimes schlocky) romances, but beneath the made-for-television veneer are some age-old, fundamental nuggets of wisdom that can help modern-day relationships, too.

Hack #1:
BE VULNERABLE

Own Your Braids

Some people may think being vulnerable is a weakness, but it's one of the strongest things you can do for yourself. Owning who you are and choosing to embrace your full self shows authenticity and invites a more genuine relationship.

Remember when adolescent Laura suddenly started skipping braids and turning on the girliness to attract the romantic interest of her pal Jimmy Hill? She didn't realize she could have remained her rough-and-tumble self, continued to hang at the fishing hole with him, *and* turned his head. She couldn't imagine her authenticity was what he liked about her in the first place.

BRAIDS GAME CHANGER: If you have fine, straight hair like Half Pint's, for best results, braid it a day or so after it's been washed rather than when it's clean. It'll be less slippery, and last longer.

Whether you're looking for a new relationship or already in a long-term commitment, being the bona fide *you* means sharing genuine emotions and feelings. Own your likes and dislikes even if some of them seem opposite from your partner's. Would you want to date someone who thinks you're a Metallica fan when it's actually Britney who tingles your Ingalls? Like with any untruth, the further you go, the deeper in it you'll get. And not even Pa has a shovel big enough to tackle that.

As a school project, Albert Ingalls began writing to a pen pal in Minneapolis. He and the girl wanted to impress each other, so she told him she was a dancer, and he shared his imagined fame as a football hero. When he showed up to surprise her, he saw that she used a wheelchair full-time, and she saw that the scrawny (but sweet) schoolboy was no sports star. After they came clean about themselves, admitting their fear that they wouldn't be accepted for who they were, they agreed to move forward as pen pals . . . honestly.

Vulnerability can be scary, but only by letting down your guard and feeling confident enough to be the genuine article do you attract who is truly meant for you. If you find yourself playing the part of someone else for the duration of your ill-fated relationship, it may not be renewed past the pilot episode.

Unpack the Hack

Own your fabulous self by upping your confidence skills! Journal about what you do well, and when you do those things, affirm yourself with positive words (spoken aloud or silently). This practice reinforces the joy in being the authentic you.

Dress, walk, and talk like you are the self-assured person you want to be, and soon you'll be strutting like Nellie Oleson on the schoolyard—though hopefully less bitchy!

Hack #2:
CULTIVATE CLARITY

Are You Canning a Peach or a Pickle?

When you've taken the time to get to know yourself and explored what you want and need from a relationship, it's easier to choose and keep a partner. Honor yourself and your authenticity by getting clear about what you want and expect from your loved one. If you're not explicit with yourself and with your significant other, little compromises will grow into big ones. Embracing clarity when it comes to love isn't always easy, but it's necessary.

There's much to consider when choosing and maintaining a romantic partnership. Are your financial, relationship, social, and even parenting values a good match? If not, you could run into trouble down the road. We saw these issues pop up and give pause even to the dynamic duo of Charles and Caroline when crops failed, grief ensued, and the repeated challenges of being a good neighbor popped up. (We're looking at you, Harriet Oleson . . . again.)

TWO'S COMPANY, THREE'S A CROWD, AND FOUR AND FIVE IS NINE.
—WILLIE OLESON
SEASON 2 • EPISODE 6 • "THE SPRING DANCE"

Although you may think you've found your perfect match, over time, you must allow the relationship to grow and change. Sometimes you find the person you love would be happier or better suited for something or someone else. We still feel sad thinking about poor Mary Ingalls and her doomed engagement with John Edwards Jr. She was truly selfless when she realized that he would have been miserable if he stayed with her in Walnut Grove to become a farmer like his father. If you love someone, you've got to let them embrace *their* clarity, and give yourself space to grieve if necessary.

What if you find yourself roped into a relationship with a nonconforming maverick? You know, the emotionally distant, trouble-causing rogues that often have a hard time with any form of commitment? Ask yourself if this is what you want. "Bad" can be sexy and thrilling because there is risk involved; when you tame something wild, it feels like an accomplishment. But make sure your intentions for the relationship match before sharing too much of your heart. On the show, Laura finally wore down Manly's commitment phobia until he realized what he wanted was marriage and family. Perhaps you've had a similar "Manly" in your life, or maybe your love interest turned out to be the perpetual bad boy who kept falling off the wagon until you told him to hit the trail. Whatever the case, be clear about what you want and then let the relationship take its course.

Another point to consider is age. Doc Baker fell in love with Kate, a much younger woman. An age difference doesn't always cause problems, but when it results in not sharing enough in common to relate to each other, it can. According to the *Atlantic* (November 2014), age *does* matter. A study they cited found that even a five-year gap makes a married couple 18 percent more likely to divorce than couples with no age gap. There are many examples of relationships where an age difference is not an issue; if you and your partner are significantly different ages, then this statistic should serve as further encouragement to foster clarity in what each of you wants and needs.

We saw a softer side of Nellie when she fell for a shoeless bumpkin, Luke. He returned her affections, and they even ran off to elope! Sadly, they realized they were just too young to be taking on such a big commitment. But seriously, what viewer didn't not-so-secretly *want* to see priss pot Nellie marry a pig farmer's son? That could have been one hell of a spin-off.

Relationships may morph over time, and none of us can fully predict their course; however, cultivating clarity as a necessary relationship tool will help keep you and your partner in sync and hopefully pointed in the right direction, together.

Unpack the Hack

It's a good idea to take some time thinking about what you want and need in love and in a partnership, which may change throughout your life. What does a good relationship look like to you? Maybe you don't want to be in a relationship at all. Sometimes we feel the pressure of society to make choices that don't feel like our own. Make a list of your priorities as an individual and make another of what you would like in a partner. When you're in a relationship, ask your partner to do the same. Compromise when you can, but stick to your guns on the values that are nonnegotiable for you, and keep in tune with yourself to know the difference.

Hack #3:
CLEARLY COMMUNICATE

Have a Fireside Chat

Why can it be so tough to communicate with a loved one, especially when the subject is difficult or triggering? Lack of self-awareness of your own needs and using old stories and strategies that no longer work are contributing factors. So is not letting yourself be vulnerable. When you state how you feel or what you need, you risk judgment and rejection.

However, if you never voice your issues, you will never have a chance of getting past them.

EVERYTHING ALWAYS LOOKS
BETTER IN THE MORNING.
—CHARLES INGALLS
SEASON 2 • EPISODE 6 • "THE SPRING DANCE"

Communication is key, but *mindfully* expressing yourself wins the blue ribbon when it comes to healthy relationships. Caroline and Charles were the perfect couple not because their relationship was void of arguments or tiffs. Remember the time Caroline put her foot down about moving yet again so the girls could attend school? Because they talked about what was bothering them, they eventually worked it out, even if it took until the end of the episode or chapter.

Often the things we get miffed about are just leftover stews that are simmering below the surface. There was an instance when Charles took a long-distance job, which meant he would be away from home for quite some time. He was so focused on the positive idea of providing for his family that he failed to understand why Caroline was upset. She wasn't hurt that he chose to go but that being separated by his absence didn't seem to bother *him*. She wanted him to say that he would have rather been home with her, that her love and happiness still mattered to him more than anything else. Even though she knew these things, it's nice to be reassured once in a while. Caroline wanted to be seen by Charles, but rather than speak up, she let her hurt feelings fester.

Take the time to think about what's going on with your thoughts, and communicate annoyances when they bubble up. You'll be less likely to take your partner's head off for leaving their sandwich crumbs on the counter when what you're really upset about is that your constant tidying up after them feels like it's taken for granted.

Like feeling seen, being heard is a critical part of healthy companionship. Create special time with no distractions to have regular conversations. This means putting down the phone or turning off the TV to look someone in the eye while they're communicating with you.

Get beyond the superficial "yes, dear" response when it comes to communicating with your partner. For especially hard or meaningful conversations, call on these other senses along with the act of purposeful listening:

+ Pay attention to where you are feeling your own emotions, and reactions to what you are hearing, in your body. Doing so helps you get a better sense of your own personal involvement in the situation.

+ Listen and speak from the heart; be respectfully honest with your feelings. Softening them doesn't help truly resolve anything.

+ Put your soul into it. It may not feel easy, but true communication comes from sharing your experiences and who you are. Be open to exploring if some of your reactions are learned behaviors that would best serve you both to investigate.

The Ingalls family may not have had our ever-present distractions of technology, but we're guessing there were times that Ma had to compete with Pa's violin noodling, or Charles had to shift Caroline's attention away from devising the best possible way to get back at Mrs. Oleson for shortchanging her in their latest egg transaction.

Letting your partner know how you're feeling isn't only important for hashing out or preventing problems; prioritizing loving communication is also an integral way of keeping the romance alive.

At one point, Isaiah says to Grace, "I never could resist your cherry pie." We'll never know if this statement was meant to be a sneaky, suggestive euphemism, but it's never a bad idea to compliment someone for something they've done that's brought you joy. Recognizing and encouraging someone with your words not only gives them warm fuzzies but also benefits you. When you are being complimentary, you create a happier and more optimistic outlook for yourself in the process.

It's easy in the day-to-day grind to forget the effort involved in keeping home and life running smoothly: the meals that are made, the home that is cleaned, the bills that are paid, the toilets that are unclogged. What about the goodnight kisses, the coffee that's always ready for you in the morning, the midday text check-ins? Be vocal about your appreciation.

....

SUFFERING PASSES WHILE LOVE IS ETERNAL.
—LAURA INGALLS WILDER

....

Communication can be fun, too. Whether they realized it or not, Laura and Almanzo created an immediate bond between them by giving each other the special names of Beth (changed from Bess in the book) and Manly. Not only can "butter biscuit" (or any cute moniker) be a funny and loving pet name for your boo, but creating code words for opportune situations can create a unique bond and get you out of some sticky situations.

You know those family get-togethers that tend to be rife with uncomfortable moments? Often one half of a couple can tolerate that awkwardness more easily than the other. If you are nodding feverishly at this example, what about coming up with an agreed-upon code word or phrase that you can use with your partner to let them know that you've reached your limit? Suddenly exclaim, "Time to make the corn bread!" or strike up a conversation about cherry pie. What would this kind of communication sound like if Laura and Manly found themselves stuck in Harriet Oleson's gossip web at the mercantile?

> **HARRIET**: *I heard Doc Baker is having a clandestine affair with Alice Garvey, and they're having secret indoor "picnics" on his exam table! What do you think about that?*

> **LAURA**: *Manly, did I leave the* squirrel stew *leftovers uncovered?*

MANLY: *We'd better go home and check. We don't want the field mice gettin' at it.*

We humans experience a wide range of emotions, and it's healthy to feel all of them, gosh darn it! Express yourself with your words and your heart—and respectfully listen. Clear, regular communication is much better than apathetic or even resentful feelings. When you bottle up resentment, it'll eventually blow harder than explosives in a rock quarry.

Unpack the Hack

Think about how you want to be heard and seen, and have a conversation about this with your partner. Ask them how *they* want to be heard and seen. Communicating about communicating—how very meta! Start being more mindful about compliments and gestures. Keep a small notebook or running doc of things your partner has mentioned that they like so the next time you're walking by a flower display or a pastry shop you know what to get them for a just-because surprise.

If expressing complex feelings verbally seems terrifying, or you're afraid you won't find the "right words," writing a letter to your partner might be a nice way to segue into the exchange. Writing allows you to take your time to make sure you are communicating your intention. Then, when your partner is sitting in front of you, you can continue the conversation with a solid base.

Hack #4:
BE PRESENT

Reap What You Sow

To maintain a healthy relationship, tend it regularly and ensure that it has what it needs to thrive. Although Mary and Adam spent a lot of time together while they worked at the school for the blind, they made space for personal check-ins with each other, visited with family, and in the evening, connected with conversation and cuddles. Staying connected and facing the world as a bonded team does wonders for your relationship.

"Dating" during pioneer time included walks, buggy rides to picnics, dancing at socials— even a little PDA at a cornhusking bee wasn't frowned upon.

Committing as a couple shouldn't mean these activities end; in fact, they become part of maintaining the relationship's vitality. It often takes conscious effort to make this happen, and a little planning and creativity can help.

Most of us are aware of the "date night" suggestion, and this tried-and-true activity is indeed an important thing to keep up when you find yourself tied down with young kids, a frantic work schedule, or even the habit of sitting around rewatching your favorite flicks.

During the pioneer era, "bundling'" wasn't having your phone, internet, and cable TV all wrapped up in a packaged deal. It was literally getting tied up in a sack so you could lie next to your potential partner under your parents' watchful eye and keep your hands to yourself!

Hey, don't get us wrong—there is something to be said for a night of "Netflix and chill," but it's also a great idea to shake things up and get yourself into new surroundings every so often. Don your best cottagecore fashion, spritz a little of your favorite scent—Miss Beadle–inspired lemon verbena, perhaps?—and make a point to spend some quality one-on-one time with your favorite person. Removing yourself from homestead distractions can make all the difference when it comes to reconnecting.

Lemon verbena isn't just for smelling; it's an ingredient used in herbal teas and even some alcoholic beverages.

It's fun when you and your partner have common interests. Laura, a tomboy at heart, taught a young man she was crushin' on the art of fishing. Find your version of a fishin' hole. Teach your honey how to play cutthroat cribbage, or ask your main squeeze to show you some sweet yoga moves.

How about packing up the wagon for a getaway? Charles took the romance reins and invited Caroline for a second honeymoon. He planned everything, including lining up the freewheeling Mr. Edwards to watch the girls in their absence. When was the last time you and your bae took a little vacay, even just an inexpensive nearby day trip? Do it!

Take a cue from the Ingalls family and book a second honeymoon—maybe to the scene of the original one. Or reenact your first date. That could be fun, weird, sexy . . . or all of the above. If we've learned anything from Charles Ingalls, it's that "fun, weird, and sexy" are sometimes a winning combination.

Although getting away is a treat, spicing up your romance doesn't require leaving town; try a new recipe and set the table for a candlelight dinner. Snuggle up for a midday matinee at the cinema, or make breakfast in bed an all-day affair.

Heat things up by using some of these aphrodisiac foods in your date-night recipes: artichokes, oysters, figs, strawberries, watermelon, chocolate, and pomegranates.

Doing the work to stay connected with your partner isn't always easy; it takes paying attention to each other's wants and needs and making the effort to prioritize the relationship.

Actor Dwayne "the Rock" Johnson once stated that his first celebrity crush was none other than Alison Arngrim, the actress who played our favorite prime-time brat Nellie Oleson.

Unpack the Hack

Create a connecting ritual for you and your "butter biscuit." Share some quiet coffee time in the morning, an afternoon walk, or an after-dinner couch cuddle to catch up and talk. This can be the ideal opportunity to make date plans, choose your next recipe, or simply share quality time to talk about everything and nothing.

Up the ante of the getaway by taking turns surprising each other with a mystery destination! The possibilities are as never-ending as Willie Oleson's trips to the outhouse.

Hack #5:
BE SELFISH (WHEN NEEDED)

Find Your Own Jam

"Selfish" gets a bad rap. Speaking up for your needs and carving out time away from your partner is not selfish, it's self-care, and it benefits your relationship. However romantic, "you complete me" is an impossible and unhealthy phrase.

Caroline kicked prairie ass when it came to meeting motherly, wifely, and household demands. Responding to her internal call, she also led the wives' walkout when many of the husbands refused to sign the petition asking for equal rights for married women. That need for independence and feeling of solidarity with the townswomen scratched an itch of Caroline's that couldn't be scratched at home. And it wasn't

Charles's responsibility to fill that need—it was his responsibility to be supportive of Caroline going out and filling it for herself.

Find your group of like-minded peeps. For some, volunteering for a political campaign or cause is fulfilling. Others may find their groove in a dance class or clubbing with friends. A healthy relationship includes time-outs for your individual growth and expansion. Some couples decide on one or two nights of the week that they each pursue their passions. It can be easier to give yourself permission to fill your bowl with "me stew" if it's scheduled ahead of time.

Even the closest couples have conversations they share only with other friends. Having outside interests and connections expands your knowledge and gives you fresh ideas to bring into the relationship. It also gives you more things to talk about than the ongoing conversation about a day at the office, the kids, or the next home honey-do.

Perhaps solitude is what's missing from your busy life. Caroline often made it seem that she couldn't last a day without her Charles around, but even she lit up at the idea of having a weekend to herself to bake pies. Too bad that alone time turned into a bacterial infection and attempted home surgery. (We would have spent the time stepping away from the stove and cooling our feet in Plum Creek.)

Dear readers, carve out time for yourselves, because unlike those who had access to Oleson's Mercantile, you can't get everything you need in one place.

Unpack the Hack

Just say yes to invitations—and initiate your own—that get you out of the house with other friends and new experiences. Encourage your SO to do the same!

Sit down with your partner and schedule a time each week that you can each pursue your separate interests. In addition to scratchin' those itches, you'll have experiences to share when you come back together.

Courtships on TV are chock-full of drama, and *Little House on the Prairie* sure milked that romance cow. But looking beyond the shiny surface of the screen and taking note of the love lessons to be learned will be udderly helpful if you decide to ride in that rodeo.

Pioneer Challenge:
MISS BEADLE'S ALLURE

We all feel more confident and attractive when we smell good, and who wouldn't want to up their game Miss Beadle–style with a little homemade lemon verbena perfume? Uplifting and revitalizing, lemon verbena has a fresh, fruity yet herbaceous scent that is both green and floral.

Creating a signature scent is easier than you'd think. All you need is a carrier oil, such as jojoba or fractionated coconut oil, a few drops of essential oil, and an apothecary bottle to mix it in. Roller bottles work great and are easily found online and wherever essential oils are sold.

You can also create a spray by mixing distilled water, witch hazel, and your essential oil into a spray bottle. The suggested ratio for a ten-ounce bottle is one cup of distilled water, half a cup of witch hazel, and ten to twenty drops of oil. The actual number of essential oil drops you add to either mixture is entirely up to you, but add slowly; a little of this concentrated oil goes a long way! A few spritzes of scented spray freshens clothing, bed linens, curtains, or a whole room.

Lemony scent not your thing? Other romantic smells include rose, neroli, ylang-ylang, jasmine, and bergamot, to name a few. Experiment and combine a few oils to make your signature concoction that will be sure to tickle someone's fancy!

PRO BLENDING TIP: Follow your nose to preview or choose your signature scent. Remove the cap(s) of your chosen oil(s) and either gently wave the bottle(s) under your nose or drop a sample on a piece of paper or a cotton swab to test the scent or scent combo.

EXTRA CREDIT: Why stop at perfume? You can add your favorite essential oil to everything from unscented lotion to massage oil.

SAFETY FIRST: Many oils can be irritating to the skin, so be careful not to apply any of them in undiluted form directly onto your skin.

CHAPTER 5
HACK YOUR FRIENDSHIPS

❖━━━━●━━━●━━━❖

DON'T BE A NELLIE

....

WELL, THERE'S A WHOLE BUNCH OF PEOPLE IN THIS WORLD
YOU DON'T KNOW YET THAT'LL BE YOUR FRIEND SOMEDAY.
—LAURA INGALLS
SEASON 4 • EPISODE 17 • "BE MY FRIEND"

....

Isn't this a comforting thought? Friends support you during tough times, celebrate you when you succeed, act as your valuable confidants, and make you laugh 'til you wet your pantaloons. When you put in the effort to be the friend you wish to have, you're more likely to strengthen your current friendships and find future ones.

As with the raising of a barn, the framework of a healthy friendship doesn't become solid and sturdy on its own. And once established, if it isn't thoughtfully maintained, the entire structure may fall into disrepair and crumble right down to its foundation.

Children rely on playtime with pals to help find a rhythm with others. This starts with simply allowing someone near—but not in—your bubble, where you learn to do the hard work of sharing and compromising. That leads to associative play, engaging with each other inside the bubble, and then eventually graduating to the intentionally coordinated effort that is cooperative play. As children, Nellie and Willie Oleson *somehow* never graduated to cooperative play.

Think about what a trusting process this is; you are allowing others to witness and eventually participate with you in your most vulnerable state. When you play, you let your guard down and your imagination soar, exposing who you are and how you think and feel.

Pioneer play included games like hide-and-seek, singing and dancing, making dolls out of corncobs or rags, and of course, our personal favorite from the *Little House in the Big Woods* book: tossing around an inflated pig bladder.

Adults rely on those skills they learned at play. Cooperation, communication, creativity, and sharing help you coexist with others at home, at work, and in your communities.

Some friendships feel easy; upon meeting, you realize you are two peas in a pod. Other friend relationships take time to grow. Friends can even become your chosen family, especially when you're not particularly close—emotionally or physically—to your own kinfolk. As you grow in age and experience, you learn that friendships require work, both to find them and to keep them going! Read on for tips and tricks straight from the prairie playground.

Hack #1:
FIND YOUR FRIENDS

Tag, They're It

How do you find a good friend? As you get older, this becomes more of a challenge. When you were young, you simply fell into a groove with someone who shared your love for dolls or kickball, and if they happened to conveniently be in the neighborhood, all the better. Common interests were easy to figure out, as the most complicated things in your life at that point were Mom force-feeding you brussels sprouts or sharing TV time with your siblings. Falling into friendship was easy.

> SHE HAD NOT KNOWN BEFORE THAT IT
> TAKES TWO TO MAKE A SMILE.
> **—LAURA INGALLS WILDER**
> *THESE HAPPY GOLDEN YEARS*

As you grow, your experience, interests, and opinions do as well, but finding commonalities remains the starting point of any friendship. It was clear to both Mary and Laura as soon as they stepped onto the schoolyard and Miss Nellie Oleson greeted them as "country girls" with scorn that this was not going to be the start of a beautiful friendship.

For women on the prairie, friendships were a necessity, as everyone counted on one another to get through tough times. Pioneer women didn't exactly have a lot of free time on their hands; their lives revolved around kid- and animal-wrangling, baking and cooking, and sewing and cleaning from sunup to sundown. Women's common interests tended to center on these tasks, which became much more pleasant when shared. Getting together with neighboring families meant the children could entertain one another, and chores like quilting and sewing went much faster.

Quilting bees began in the nineteenth century and were a way for women to gather and share news, gossip, and friendship while they worked. A *bee* is another word for a party or social function, so a quilting bee is another way of saying "quilting party," although it, of course, had a totally different vibe from a barn dance social.

Like pioneer men and women, modern folks bond at the workplace. Whether it's in an office or through our computer screens, sharing creative projects and solving problems together are great opportunities to create friendships that go beyond our nine-to-fives. Think of all the times Charles and Isaiah had lunchtime discussions about the perks and problems of family life over a boiled potato!

There was no swapping Twinkies for Cheetos back in Walnut Grove. Their pails more than likely held bread and lard, hard-boiled eggs, some dried fruit, or a boiled potato, if they were lucky. Their drink was double-dipping a ladle into a shared bucketful of well water. Pass the germs, please.

How do you discover friends now? Sometimes you simply find one another. It's like your energies connect and you recognize something of yourself in someone else. Maybe you're at a party and you hear someone mention something about baking with rhubarb and the friendship light goes on, encouraging you to approach them to further discuss all things rhubarb. In that conversation, you learn you both also love facial hair, chai tea, and collecting buttons. Instant friendship!

Most of the time, however, you'll have to actively seek others with whom you share interests. It's time to think outside the sandbox and get creative as to how you can widen that circle of friends. Start hanging out where you know you'll run into potential pals. Are you a crafter? Strike up conversations in the bead aisle of your favorite craft store. Love to read? Find a community book club. Like to walk? Connect with a walking buddy through a neighborhood message board or social media group. Have you always been curious about *Dungeons & Dragons*? There are many gaming stores with people just waiting for your dragonborn paladin to join their campaign.

But what if you don't work with others or live in a busy community? In Walnut Grove, folks connected at church functions, local fairs, or maybe by grabbing for the same package of stove polish at the mercantile.

The mercantile, or general store, was often a hub of social interaction. People hung out there listening for gossip, discussing baking or farming, and admiring the newest products that'd arrived. In the 1800s, you would not only find staples like eggs, soaps, and clothing in one of these stores, but also be offered strange elixirs that were mostly alcohol (sometimes mercury!) and claimed to cure such ailments as stomach, lung, or blood diseases. If those cures didn't work, you could have even picked up a coffin or two!

Today, even if you don't find yourself in a close community with others, a new friend may be just a click or phone call away. Push yourself to join online groups that give you a chance to share your love for geek culture or quilting. Before you know it, you'll be stitchin' and bitchin' with others in no time.

If social media had been around in the pioneer days, we're pretty sure Mary would have been active in a group like "Rule Followers," and Nellie would have created her own fan page. Nels would pretend like he didn't care about social media, but we think he'd secretly be comparing sale prices of assorted sundries . . . and studying Charles's inspirational Instagram quotes to help him manage his dysfunctional family. #blessed

Make an effort to connect. If someone you admire writes a blog or records a podcast, read, listen, and comment. If they post a photo in their latest fancy go-to-meetin' garb and you think they look fabulous, tell them. Join the conversation, get involved! Support someone's small business, and become their biggest fan by sharing what you love about them. People recognize and appreciate that love, and many will be eager to give it right back. This makes it easy to take the connection out of the cloud and right down into your everyday life.

No matter where you meet new friends, don't forget to check yourself for authenticity. Are you showing potential friends your true self, or are you pretending to share interests so you'll be liked? Although it may seem like the fast track to friendship, the truth will eventually reveal itself and could cause you to lose that friend. As Laura and her buddy Jonah discovered, when you pan for gold, you sometimes end up with bags and bags of pyrite. Fool's gold may trick some, but it's just a bag of rocks. Don't be a bag of rocks.

Unpack the Hack

Expand your friend group. Is there an interest you don't share with *any* of your current friends? Be brave and take a class or attend an event solo to learn more about that interest. While you're there, strike up conversations with others regarding the subject. You may surprise yourself with a newfound pal with which to enjoy this particular pursuit!

But don't neglect your core friend group! Take a cue from our hardworking pioneer pals: Throw a yard-cleaning party, make a grocery shopping playdate, and engage in a little parallel play by tackling a task side by side with a friend.

Hack #2:
SIMON SAYS, ACCEPT THE RISKS

Seek, Don't Hide

Finding those cool friends that are the bees to your knees is just the beginning. Being vulnerable and earning someone's trust is what really makes a friendship blossom. Most people want friends who will place their private conversations in their vault and not share them with every Lars, Doc, and Mary.

If you want to be able to trust your friends, you must first show you're trustworthy. Being vulnerable has burned each of us at some point, but building trust requires it.

Laura trusted Nellie (her first mistake) and told her about her crush on the newest prairie hottie, Jason. Nellie also fancied him and, in typical Nellie fashion, put Half Pint through the mill by getting her to admit the crush and then secretly recording it on her newfangled "talking machine." As if that weren't catty enough, Nellie then played it in front of the entire class. Talk about soul-crushing!

Mr. Edwards didn't inspire trust in Ma because she judged his book by the ratty old cover. To be fair, Isaiah Edwards did look (and probably smelled) like he washed his face with a frying pan and combed his hair with a wagon wheel. He became Pa's BFF, and Charles constantly tried to convince Caroline of his hidden virtues. When the Ingalls family was financially strapped at Christmastime, he braved a blizzard and came through with gifts for Mary, Laura, and Carrie. This was the proof Ma needed that he could be a trustworthy friend.

Vulnerability is a gift to others. Any time you open yourself up to someone else, it makes the relationship that much more meaningful and genuine. A true friend is someone you can be your less-than-perfect self with and invite over when your barn is full of manure and your kitchen is a mess. When you air your dirty laundry with them, they know they can put theirs out on the line with you.

Unpack the Hack

Have a conversation with a friend and share something you haven't before, which may prompt your friend to do the same. If they do, validate and support them in making that connection. Just try not to pick anyone with a headful of golden curls, a collection of French dolls, and a name that rhymes with Shmellie.

Passing notes doesn't only happen in the schoolhouse. If past betrayals make it tough to speak up, write an email or a note, and then make a follow-up date to talk about it.

Isaiah's happy song was "Old Dan Tucker," and he sang it often. Its origins aren't clear, but it wasn't written for the show. The first sheet music for it was published in 1843. Verse:

Old Dan Tucker was a fine old man

Washed his face with a fryin' pan

Combed his hair with a wagon wheel

And died with a toothache in his heel

Hack #3:
KEEP YOUR COOL

When You're Not on the Same Slate

We all have times when we need to force ourselves to get along with someone who isn't exactly our cup of chamomile tea.

The miffs between Caroline and Harriet were legendary; you couldn't find two people more different from each other than they were. Ma's steadfast patience was tested with Harriet's ongoing belittling, gossiping, and bickering. Despite their constant tension, when the time came for them to move apart, each realized they were going to miss the other. Caroline and Harriet may not have been what we would call good friends, but they went through a lot together and shared plenty of history.

Children are usually taught to be nice to the kids in their class, even the ones they don't mesh with. As you get out into the world and away from your comfort zones, you're constantly dealing with people who are a part of your life out of necessity: colleagues who would not be on your dance card, a nosy neighbor who's always up in your business (hello, Harriet!), your friend's college pal who just rubs you the wrong way. It can be tricky to find that balance of amicable indifference. You don't have to be friends with everyone, but you can do your best to get along. Try to focus on the good qualities of the thorn in your side.

Speaking of bullies: Walnut Grove's own Nellie Oleson. Remember, a thorn is on the stem of a beautiful rose out of protection for itself; the rose is fragile and wants to keep pickers and smellers at a safe distance. More than likely, someone's prickliness has nothing to do with you, but experiences in their past left them feeling wary. Take a deep breath and then the high road; you may be surprised where it leads you.

Sometimes, no matter how much you want to give someone the benefit of the doubt, you need to keep certain people on the periphery. Bullies aren't only in the schoolyard; we still deal with them as adults. If you've gotten this far in life without being bullied in one way or another, count yourself lucky, because you're a damn unicorn. Although you know a bully's behavior stems from their insecurities, their jabs still hurt.

Nellie's family owned the mercantile; they were, as she said, "the richest family in town!" Having money didn't make her a sourpuss—her father, Nels, was as down-to-earth as they came. Her mother, Harriet, on the other hand . . . let's just say the bad apple didn't fall far from the tree. She spoiled Nellie and told her she was better than everyone. So naturally, Nellie wound up sharing her mother's attitude with anybody and everybody.

On-screen, Nellie and Laura were like oil and water, but when the camera wasn't rolling, Alison Arngrim and Melissa Gilbert were the best of friends and are still close today.

If we listed all the examples of Nellie acting like a bully, this chapter would be longer than the Oregon Trail. Because nasty people make for good drama, the *Little House on the Prairie* show gave us plenty of opportunities to see how our favorite characters dealt with the various tyrants and ruffians that crossed their dusty paths.

Nellie particularly got under Laura's skin, and Half Pint wasn't afraid to speak her mind for better or for worse. Sometimes her fiery temper got the best of her, and she chose to settle the score with a round of mud wrestling in the creek. Sweet little Half Pint kept giving sourpuss Nellie another chance, but that consistently left Laura's glass half-empty. Eventually, she listened to her parents' advice and ignored Nellie.

What *is* the best way to handle bullying behavior? As adults, we may find ourselves intimidated by a boss, an aggressive salesperson, a friend or family member, or even a romantic partner. Thankfully, you're the only one who can choose your response. And that's the first rule: Respond, don't react. Calmly speak your mind and tell them that you don't appreciate and won't put up with that kind of behavior. The exception is if the bully is acting aggressively—then you should immediately remove yourself from the situation and find safety. However, if it's someone trying to get your goat, often the best thing to do is ignore them and go about your business. If there's one thing bullies hate, it's being ignored. Speaking of goats and bullies, wasn't it satisfying when Fred the drunk goat kicked Harriet Oleson in the tuchus? We digress . . .

Sometimes you need to completely break free from a toxic person. This may mean quitting your job, splitting up with a partner, ending a friendship, or even discontinuing a relationship with a family member. That's tough—but continually remind yourself that you are responsible for your well-being and that life *without* that person is healthier than *with* them.

> Fans were surprised when the town of Walnut Grove was blown up on the finale episode, "The Last Farewell," on March 21, 1983. In a *New York Times* article the previous month, Michael Landon said, "I think it makes for a good strong pioneer ending. It was also a nice catharsis for the cast and crew. There were lots of tears when we finally blew up the town. The actors had all become very attached to their own buildings, so it was very emotional."

When you start the conversation to put a kibosh on a friendship, it's best if you can maintain the focus on yourself and your feelings. Staying calm without playing the blame game will keep your friend off the defensive.

If you are able, end the conversation on a positive note, remembering the good times that you shared. To achieve resolution and move on, try your best to keep revenge thoughts to a minimum. Making a rash decision like destroying an entire town probably wasn't the best path to inner peace, but we're guessing the fictional Walnut Grove residents didn't get that memo. Thankfully, they never knew, but at least the cast members did!

When a friend is cut loose or just drifts away, they sometimes find their way back to you. If they had been truly toxic, you'll want to make sure that they've done the work on themselves and are ready to bring a healthier outlook to your friendship. Ultimately, you get to decide if you want them back on the playground. Who has time for those games?

Unpack the Hack

To practice keeping your cool, begin a simple, daily meditation. Start by sitting still, clearing your mind, and/or listening to a guided recording for just five minutes a day. Meditation can help you more quickly get to a place of calmness that may help in tough friend encounters—or any of life's aggravations! Don't be too hard on yourself if it feels impossible to sit still and clear your mind. It's called a *practice* for a reason. Eventually, you'll feel as cool as a shirtless Pa on a summer's day. Well, none of us will ever be *that* cool.

Meditation doesn't have to be sitting around in the lotus position and chanting, "Om." Get out and walk or take a drive; clearing your mind can take many forms, so find the one that works for you.

Hack #4:
FEED YOUR FRIENDSHIP

Balancing the Teeter-Totter

Friendship starts from within. Are you doing your part to keep your relationship in line? If you take a good, long look at yourself, are you more of a Laura or Nellie kind of friend? Nellie was a brat because she was allowed to be. Until Percival came along, no one had ever held her accountable for her actions. Sometimes we make poor decisions out of fear and insecurity or because we've never been taught or shown what it takes to be a good friend. Okay, so the show kind of lost some of its fun when Nellie got nice, but in real life, less drama between friends is always a good thing! Maintaining a solid friendship is a two-person job, and you can only control your part.

Charles was great pals with both Isaiah Edwards and Jonathan Garvey and sometimes offered to share paid gigs with one of them when their finances were tight. Not only did they each get a paycheck, but they also got to spend time together while long-hauling lumber or working side by side at the mill. All this time together left room for conversation about families, struggles, practical life advice, and maybe even floppy boot repair.

Some friends are only in your life for a season or two (or for one episode, like the many great new "friends" on the show who were prominent in one episode yet never showed up in the church pew again). You know this drill . . . you've always gotten along just fine with your buddy and stayed connected in one way or another until, suddenly, you didn't. When Mary had to say goodbye to John Jr. and the engagement was off, she not only lost a fiancé, she lost a friend. Their interests and values diverged, and their relationship was too strained to remain friendly.

FRIENDSHIP ELIXIR: Create a signature cocktail unique to you and your friend(s). Use two parts liquor of your choice, one part sweet (simple syrup, honey, maple syrup), and one part sour (lemon or lime). And don't forget the garnish (sprig of an herb like rosemary or even an edible flower). If you don't drink alcohol, skip the liquor in favor of seltzer and make it a mocktail. Remember to name your new drink!

But for those pals who stick around, what does it take to ensure that you're giving your friendships your best? Friendship requires grace. Life demands a lot, and it's easy to narrow our focus only on ourselves; being a graceful buddy means looking beyond yourself. Celebrate the moments in your friends' lives, both big and small. Be the one who organizes a happy hour for your bestie who nailed a promotion. Stock up on thoughtful greeting cards so you have some on hand when you want to let a pal know you're thinking about them.

When families moved to reap the benefits of rich farmland, they often left dear friends behind. To ease the pain of separation and serve as a remembrance gift, women sometimes created a friendship quilt for the departing woman.

Cards and "I saw this and thought of you" little prezzies are wonderful ways to show a friend just how special they are to you, but the most important gift you can give a pal is your time and attention. Extend the effort to send a text or make that quick call just to say howdy. These are ways you feed a friendship. Even when the Walnut Grove families had to temporarily relocate to Winoka and were so busy creating their new lives, the adult friends would find time to come together at the hotel restaurant at the end of their busy days.

WELL, WE'RE ALL STRANGERS, BOY, UNTIL WE BECOME FRIENDS.
—NELS OLESON
SEASON 4 • EPISODE 19 • "THE STRANGER"

Don't be completely selfless. Too often, we find ourselves becoming so immersed in work and our family relationships that we forget to make time to explore and discover our interests. As your life changes and evolves, what you enjoy can change, too. Are you doing things just out of habit? Or passively going along with the interests of others without being more assertive with your desires? When you don't make your pastimes a priority, you find yourself feeling as empty as Nellie's promises to be a good friend.

Like any kind of relationship, a friendship can have more ups and downs than a seesaw. You get to decide if that ride is something you want to continue or if you want to hop off and play elsewhere, with someone else.

Unpack the Hack

Create your own version of "Sisterhood of the Traveling Bonnet." Find something to pass between friends—this can be done between two pals or an entire group. Maybe a pair of sunglasses, a lucky bracelet, a plant, or a cake pan that you must fill before you pass it to the next person? Or how about a traveling scrapbook, wherein each person adds a memento before handing it off? It could include takeout menus, stickers, bar coasters, and loads of inside jokes. Can you envision the scrapbook that would have been passed between Caroline and Alice Garvey? We're imagining pages of stained pie recipes, scraps of calico, and Oleson's Mercantile receipts for matching ladles.

Pioneer Challenge:
CONTAIN YOUR FRIENDSHIP

Looking for a thoughtful gift for your bestie? Fill a fun jar, box, or any type of container with friendship memories, inside jokes, pick-me-ups, and heartfelt messages—write each one on a small piece of paper and fold it up. Place them inside the container for your friend to draw one whenever they think of it. Each time they read one of the little messages, they'll be reminded of you and the experiences you've shared.

This project has Mary Ingalls written all over it, and we think she'd have made these for friends and study buddies. Her messages might have been . . .

> *"I am not afraid of storms for I am learning to sail my ship."* —Louisa May Alcott, *Little Women*

> *"IOU one homemade calico bonnet when we next meet!"*

> *"I still think of that time we were studying for the geography test and Albert threw a piece of potato at our book and it landed on Oklahoma."*

This gift doesn't have to be just for friends. Make one for Mother's Day, Valentine's Day, anniversaries, holy holidays, or on a "just because" day.

EXTRA CREDIT: Decorate the outside of the container with photos of the two of you together, greeting card covers, wrapping paper from a gift you previously exchanged, or any mementos that would easily stick to the outside of the box or jar.

CHAPTER 6

HACK YOUR WORK LIFE

DON'T REINVENT THE WAGON WHEEL

HARDWORKING FOLKS ONLY SMELL BAD TO FOLKS THAT HAVE
NOTHING TO DO BUT STICK THEIR NOSES IN THE AIR!
—LAURA INGALLS
SEASON 2 • EPISODE I • "THE RICHEST MAN IN WALNUT GROVE"

A work life that's fulfilling, balanced, full of passion, and even playful exists beyond a TV screen or the pages of a book. With a little moxie and some home-grown inspiration from the fine folks of Walnut Grove, *you* can create that career for yourself.

Pa Ingalls was always spouting his Aristotelian wisdom about the virtue of challenging work, but going by Laura's quote above, he may not have gotten a whiff of someone after a strenuous workout. There is a waft of truth to what she's saying, though; we get a healthy satisfaction in the stink that comes from a hard day's work, whether that be plowing the field, stress-sweating over a new proposal, or even that grueling CrossFit session. (Don't forget a good deodorant!)

Of course, many people spend the workweek looking forward to weekends of cocktails and backyard parties, but most everyone likes to work in *some* shape or form. Ideally, working can make you feel productive, useful, skilled, and hopefully like you are contributing to something bigger than yourself, in addition to helping you pay your rent and keeping the lights on. It can give you a sense of pride and accomplishment to see the finished product of a task you've started from the very beginning.

There wasn't one person who could survive prairie life without putting in the work. Pa not only farmed his lands and was the quintessential Mr. Fix-It but also held down a second job at the mill. Ma was always whipping up nutritious home-cooked meals, washing clothes, corralling the children, and keeping up the house, farm, and garden—and then she went and added a full-time job running the kitchen at the restaurant. Every kid helped with various chores and tended to the animals. No one had the luxury of letting any of these things go for very long; no crops meant no food, and a crowded little house would get very cluttered, dirty, and downright unlivable if everyone wasn't chipping in to keep it clean.

But what do you do when you just aren't feeling it? When just the thought of having to organize that work meeting, weed that garden, or fix that broken wagon wheel feels overwhelming and you don't want to lift a modern-ass finger? Pull up your crinolines and read on.

Hack #1:
ALMOST EVERYTHING IS A CHOICE

To Churn or Not to Churn

Did you know that you actually don't *have* to do anything? You don't have to brush your teeth, whip up tonight's dinner, or even go to work.

Imagine waking up like Pa might've on a chilly morning in the little house, toasty and warm under the calico quilt, thinking about your seemingly endless chores for the day: plowing the damn field, and then running over to sweat some more at the mill. All to come home and toss some hay bales, fix the wagon wheel (again), help the kids with their schoolwork, and *then* keep the family entertained with a bedtime story or a faddle on the fiddle. Think about waking up as Ma, and knowing your entire day was going to be making biscuits from scratch, scouring the outhouse, hand-sewing your whole family's wardrobe, scrubbing Pa's ever-present sweat stains out on the washboard, making yet *another* meal, doing the dishes, sweeping the floor, and finally flopping back onto your straw bed. Or even imagine being one of the Ingalls girls, stretching awake in your sleeping cap knowing you have to trudge out on the long walk to school, sometimes during a freakin' snowpocalypse, as "country girls" trying to keep up with the town kids and dealing with Nellie Oleson's constant bitchery? It's enough to make prairie folks want to collapse into the tub to wash away the day—except a relaxing soak for all but Pa meant sometimes hanging out in secondhand bathwater.

Pioneers usually had two sets of work clothes—one to wear and the other to air out. Laundry was done once a week.

The Ingalls family could have easily decided to skip it all for a day . . . just sleep in and have pancakes for supper. But each one of them knew that if they ignored their chores and studies, they'd be dealing with the consequences that came with that choice: no money from the harvest, an overflowing outhouse, and no opportunity to outsmart those unbearable Olesons.

Chores may look different now, but you, too, have a choice with most things that you do. Sure, you could skip brushing your teeth, for example, but doing that too often could cause you a mouthful of tooth trouble and perhaps a bad case of halitosis. You could skip making dinner, but eating bowls of cereal every night would get old really fast, as would spending all your hard-earned cash on takeout Thai.

Don't underestimate the simple glory of pancakes for supper—or any other breakfast fare, for that matter. These meals are often made with easy ingredients we tend to have around the house, so they're a no-fuss choice after an especially busy workday. (Maybe a bowl of Lucky Charms isn't the most nutritious choice, but we all have those days!)

Even whether you climb out of your organically mattressed bed in a climate-controlled bedroom to haul your butt into work is your decision; you could certainly choose to be a professional wanderer instead, traveling the country in floppy-soled boots, risking your life hitching rides, and eating questionable mushrooms. Some people do choose to live off the grid and are perfectly happy doing so, but most people probably like having the predictability of a roof over their heads and proper food on the table, so they *choose* to go to the office or clock in on their computer.

The most common way pioneers cleaned their teeth was with a little "brush" made by fraying the end of a birch twig. They also used dental powders made from combining strange ingredients like burnt eggshell ashes and animal hooves.

When you realize that you are making a choice to do the things you do in every moment of every day, you feel more in control of your life. You see the bigger picture and know that you are the one with the power to create the life you want to live. Doesn't that feel better? Especially when you realize your "outhouse duty" only involves flushing a nice modern toilet.

Unpack the Hack

Start paying attention to whenever you complain or start dreading that you "have to" do something, and substitute "choose to" instead. How does this change your attitude about it?

The distance from the Ingalls family's house on Plum Creek to the schoolhouse in downtown Walnut Grove was three miles—quite a hike in a blustery Minnesota winter!

Hack #2:
DETERMINE WHAT MAKES YOU TICK

What Drives Your Buggy?

Other than the physical consequences of a stinky loo and no cash on the barrel, it's pretty clear that family was Ma and Pa's main motivation for all the hard work they endured every day. Hard work feels like nothing but drudgery when there isn't a reason behind it. Looking past the daily grind and keeping your eyes on the prize helps you get through it a bit easier.

Having your *why* not only helps you move toward your goals but also gives you the gumption to keep going. When there's something you really want, you can bet your biscuits that it'll sometimes be a rickety ride; life generally throws plenty of rocks and wide streams on your path. Whenever you have to really work for something, the sweet reward is often well worth the struggle.

> **LAURA:** Is gumption a gift?
>
> **PA:** It sure is. —Season 1 • Episode 7 • "Town Party, Country Party"

When the Ingalls family's wheat was destroyed by hail, Pa took exactly one moment to feel sorry for himself and then decided he was going to trudge as far as he could to find work. Turns out it was about one hundred miles, in worn-out boots with deteriorating soles. Because of his love for his family, he had his *why*. He knew that he needed to replace the value of what they'd lost, and that it wasn't going to magically appear from him just sitting around crying among his crops. He said, *Hail no!* to that, pulled himself up by his floppy bootstraps, and got moving in a different direction.

> In the summer of 1875, real-life Charles Ingalls lost his wheat to a bumper crop of Rocky Mountain locusts that not only destroyed the fields but literally chewed the clothes right off a woman's body.

What gets your wagon wheels rollin'? Sure, a paycheck at the end of the week is a major motivator, but to feel really fulfilled in our work, we must think bigger than the Benjamins. Look beyond the everyday Instagram snapshots of your perfectly frothed lattés or that on-trend outfit that having a job affords you and think about your bigger picture.

Unpack the Hack

Take some time in your busy life to stop running in circles and tag yourself—you're it! What are you working toward? What dreams would you be willing to walk one hundred miles to make a reality? Meditate on this—do some journaling. Create a physical or online vision board with images of whatever your *why* is and look at it every day.

WASH ON MONDAY, IRON ON TUESDAY, MEND
ON WEDNESDAY, CHURN ON THURSDAY, CLEAN ON FRIDAY,
BAKE ON SATURDAY, REST ON SUNDAY.
—LAURA INGALLS WILDER
LITTLE HOUSE IN THE BIG WOODS

Hack #3:
HACK THOSE TASKS

Let the Barn Raising Begin!

You've figured out what your choices are, and the *why* of why you're prepared to work so hard. Now you need to figure out just how to do it. At times, you likely find yourself staring at a bushel of work and feeling mighty overwhelmed.

Pay attention to when you do your best work. Because of their unpredictable farm life, the Ingalls family often didn't have the luxury of scheduling exactly when Pa would plant the wheat or when the chickens would lay enough eggs for Ma to sell to the mercantile. With your more modern conveniences, you can and should take advantage of how you work best and create that environment for yourself as often as you can, especially as many of us have learned to work from home when modern-day plagues and pestilence require it. Before you start plowing through that to-do list, think about what each task entails and how you will be the most productive.

If it's something that feels icky or overwhelming, maybe it's better to do it another day or not even do it at all. Sometimes you are actually more productive if you blow something off to focus on other things that give you momentum or even added motivation. Maybe putting off that meeting until tomorrow could *help* your deadline. Perhaps crossing "mop the floor" off your list gives you time to simply sit and relax, which refreshes you and makes the rest of the day that much better.

> IF ENOUGH PEOPLE THINK OF A THING AND WORK
> HARD ENOUGH AT IT, I GUESS IT'S PRETTY NEARLY BOUND
> TO HAPPEN, WIND AND WEATHER PERMITTING.
> —LAURA INGALLS
> *BY THE SHORES OF SILVER LAKE*

Back on the prairie, folks rarely—if ever—had the opportunity to toss a task onto the back burner. If you postpone writing a work report by a day or two, there probably won't be dire consequences; however, if Pa put off repairing a wagon wheel, he could've missed an important lumber delivery to Sleepy Eye that he'd promised Mr. Hanson. Nobody wants a lumber catastrophe on their hands.

Sometimes the best way to deal with a task is to give it to someone else or, if finances allow, pay a service to do it for you. Maybe that meeting has always been yours to initiate and lead, but delegating it to someone else could take it off your busy plate and also give that person a chance to shine. Getting groceries delivered gives you one less thing to think about when you are losing sleep with your newborn baby or up all night studying for exams.

There are tasks that are downright impossible to put off or have someone else do for you, so how can you make those better? Do you have a particularly busy day ahead of you? Ditch the usual brown bag and treat yourself to your favorite takeout.

Scared to death of the dentist? Go ahead of time to get a lay of the land and have your questions answered. Bring a friend along or listen to relaxing music during the drilling process. At least you know that Doc Baker won't be coming after you with a pair of pliers!

Get creative and find ways to make that task-mastering choice the most fun and best it can possibly be. Picture what it will feel like to have done it. And then bask in the glory of the fact that you faced it head-on and are now able to punctuate it with a satisfying check mark.

Unpack the Hack

Examine your upcoming dreaded tasks and how each one will affect your day. Is it better to delay it? Farm it out to someone else? If you know that you and you alone are the one to get it done, how can you make that task the best it can be?

Hack #4:
TALK THE TALK AND WALK THE WALK

Get a Bee in Your Bonnet

On the TV show, young Laura Ingalls wanted to be a teacher. From day one in the little schoolhouse, any fears she had were quickly quelled by discovering her love of learning (and Miss Beadle's lemon verbena perfume). Her love of school soon grew into an obsession, which led her to want to teach and inspire others. This is what drove Laura's buggy, but she didn't park there quietly. She was vocal about her passion, proclaiming her goal out loud to herself and her family with a toothy grin.

According to the books, however, Laura's main inspiration for earning her teaching certificate was so that she could contribute to Mary's college tuition. In either case, she'd decided she was going to get that credential permission slip, come heck or high creek. She studied hard and, despite some meddling Nellie roadblocks, reached that goal.

A female schoolteacher in 1885 earned an average salary of $54.50 a year. Accounting for inflation, that's a little more than $1,600 in 2022.

Half Pint shows us that it's never too soon (or too late) to dream your dreams. But you can't just dream; you've gotta act.

Unpack the Hack

Create motivation and accountability for yourself and others by sharing your goals and dreams. Bonus: You've created your own cheering section!

What small steps can you take to commit to that goal?

Hack #5:
TAKE CARE OF YOURSELF

Don't Neglect Your Daily Constitutional

It is the way of our society to work ourselves into the ground in the name of reaching success. Beware of creating a life that's all work and no play. If you never make the time for a mental break to relax at your favorite fishing hole like a young Half Pint or enjoy that game of ring-around-the-rosy, your work will take its toll.

> The kids of Walnut Grove played endless games of ring-around-the-rosy in the schoolyard. Folklore says the ring in ring-around-the-rosy is a rash that's common in some forms of the plague; the posies were carried to ward off the disease or hide the smell of it; "ashes-ashes, we all fall down" referred to death by plague—fun, right?

Additionally, getting in some kind of daily exercise is important. Life on the prairie provided endless natural opportunities to be active. Just walking to work and school got their steps in without relying on a Fitbit, and there surely weren't bingeable episodes of *Martha & Snoop's Potluck Dinner Party* to tempt them into becoming couch taters.

Looking Instagram-ready wasn't the Ingalls family's incentive for keeping fit; it was simply a natural part of their lifestyle and helped them keep up with their strenuous life on the farm and prairie. To Ma, spinning was more about wool than exercise, and Pa would have likely thought that a "treadmill" meant treading to the mill to put in a hard day's work.

In this modern age, for so many of us, the only exercise our day-to-day life requires is walking from the fridge to the couch, the parking lot to the office, or skillfully maneuvering an overly laden shopping cart through crowded grocery store aisles. An active body not only keeps you limber and strong but also supplies your brain with oxygen, which promotes the production of new brain cells that help create new synapses. With this, your productivity and focus only get sharper! A healthier body and mind fill your soul so that you can do your best work, rest, and play.

It's also easy to get so caught up working our daily jobs and doing chores that we forget to make the time to rest. Ma understood this and called Pa out for plowing the fields on "the Lord's Day" when he should have been resting. He knew that if he gave his oxen and horses a good rest when they needed it, the animals would haul the plow and pull their wagon more efficiently. It's a simple fact: You can't show up in your work life 100 percent if you don't honor the need to prop your boots up once in a while.

Resting is your time to recharge! It's not just your nightly Zs we are talking about here—rests can be mental, too. Taking even five minutes for a quiet breather can make all the difference in a busy workday. When you take slow, deep breaths, you activate your parasympathetic nervous system, which decreases your heart rate and helps to lower your blood pressure. Even Mr. Oleson had to step aside and take breathers—maybe that was mostly because of the chaos Mrs. Oleson, Nellie, and Willie brewed up, but we're sure it also positively affected his workday.

Remember that you are never too old to play! Play is a way children learn. When the Ingalls kids went fishing, they learned about nature and living things. Whenever they played tag or softball, they discovered valuable lessons about being humble in both winning and losing.

This still holds true for us even as we age, and "play" becomes "hanging out." Socializing brings healthy laughter and exposure to new stimuli. The variety of activities that make up your free time gives you opportunities to learn more about yourself and others. Not only are these learning benefits important, but there's also pure magic-making that comes from doing something that simply inspires joy and lets off some steam. Pa (and his fiddle) would definitely endorse this message.

Life is all about balance. We never stop learning and growing, so we should never stop moving, resting, playing, and keeping our bodies as healthy as they can be. All these things make you more productive, and life's just too short to not get the most out of every minute.

Unpack the Hack

How will you take some time to move, play, and rest today? Here are some ideas:

- Move: Get up from your chair and move every thirty to sixty minutes, use a standing desk, and/or take a lunchtime walk. Did you know that you are more likely to get an aha moment when you are walking? Double-whammy bonus!
- Play: Make a list of things you've been wanting to do, and do them: Hit that museum, take that pottery class, see that movie. Make a coffee or happy hour date with a friend or family member. Play Frisbee on a sunny day and video games when you'd rather be inside.
- Rest: Do a five-minute breathing exercise or meditation, read a chapter of your favorite book, take that nap, turn everything off, make a cup of tea, and just be.

Schedule these things into your day—or at least your week—so they become a priority and a regular part of your life.

Hack #6:
BRING THE PLAY TO WORK

Harvest Some Fun

BUT I DO LOVE TO WORK. AND IT IS A PLEASURE TO WRITE FOR THE
MISSOURI RURALIST. OH AND I DO JUST LOVE TO PLAY!
—LAURA INGALLS WILDER
FARM JOURNALIST: WRITINGS FROM THE OZARKS

You know the old "Whistle While You Work" song that the seven dwarves sang in Disney's *Snow White* tale? Whistling "Old Dan Tucker" in the office or during a Zoom meeting could be pretty disruptive, but there are plenty of other ways to make your workday more fun and fulfilling.

Some of us are extremely lucky and get to incorporate our passions into our workdays. But for others, it can be tough to slog through the daily menial to-dos, feeling as though weekends or vacations are the only opportunities to have fun or spend time stoking the creative fires.

Some feel that work is more fun with fellow employees nearby, but with so many of us telecommuting these days, we miss out on that camaraderie. Why not work side by side? If you can, meet up at a coffee shop or take turns setting up in one another's home office. If that doesn't work, there are plenty of online coworking options where you can "hang out" together!

Horse manure! Perhaps you're an avid flower gardener and spend hours planting, nurturing, and admiring the flower beds in your yard. At work, you're constantly showing coworkers the latest images of your thriving Montauk daisies or the blue-ribbon potential of your beautifully blooming zinnias. While you're at your desk, you find your mind wandering to thoughts of deadheading and fertilizing. Is it possible to bring your passion for flowers into your work environment? Why not? Perhaps adding a couple of potted flowers to your desk area would do the trick, or lining your cubicle walls with "proud parent" photos of your own garden would lighten your mood and make your job more fun. Who knows, maybe you'd get a raise because your boss notices your increased positivity and flood of new ideas in the latest brainstorming meeting. Anything is possible when you think outside the (flower) box.

Unpack the Hack

What project, deadline, or menial work task is looming over you that has you dreading it more than discovering rats in the cornmeal? How can you add your very own twist to make it more enjoyable and meaningful to you and to others?

Whether you have a conventional career, are part of the gig economy, or your commendable full-time job is caring for children, hearth, and home, work is an integral part of your contemporary life. It's time for you to take a closer look at what you do and make some decisions. Do you even want to continue on your current path? Do you have the option to make major changes, or will small changes make a big difference? Charles Ingalls said, "What must be done is best done cheerfully." We have choices, and we can make them with a joyful, grateful heart.

Making their own choices, getting intentional, understanding how they could be their most productive selves, and having work-life balance seemed to come so naturally to our beloved Ingalls family. Imagine how fulfilling it would be to realize that whatever you're working on is finally working for *you*? Let's try to follow their lead by hacking away at the perceived drudgery of daily work to embrace it more as a working lifestyle.

We think Pa would approve, giving you a nod of his head and a twinkle in his eye, along with his admiration for your well-earned sweat.

Prairie Challenge:
COMMUTE AND COMMUNE

The global pandemic brought not only challenges but changes as well. One of the biggest was the number of us who started working from home on a full-time basis and therefore giving up our commutes to and from office locations.

Where this is generally viewed as a positive transformation, many also found that they missed that alone time their commute offered to jam to tunes, listen to their favorite podcast, mentally prep for that dreaded meeting, or merely zone out to get some reflective time in before and after their busy day.

Even if you never had a commute or hated every minute of it, there is something to be said for starting or ending your day with extra time to do whatever it is that makes you happy, just for you. Set your alarm a little earlier and take the time to "commute and commune" before starting your day. Or create time at the end of your workday to decompress. It may very well help you feel more in control of your time.

CHAPTER 7
HACK YOUR SELF-CARE

◆▬◆ ◆▬◆ ◆▬◆

SOMETIMES YOU'VE GOTTA BE THE
FIRST IN THE BATHWATER

....

YOU KNOW, THERE'S ONLY ONE THING IN THE WORLD
YOU CAN DO BETTER THAN ANYONE ELSE. JUST BE YOURSELF.
—PA INGALLS
SEASON 4 • EPISODE 2 • "TIMES OF CHANGE"

....

The pioneers' days were taxing, with physical work from sunup to sundown. They didn't think of work as exercise, or that exercise was self-care, but it certainly was. (Imagine the bewildered looks that would become fits of laughter at the mention of "self-care" to the Ingalls family.) Even spoiled Harriet Oleson worked her bustled tail off, wheeling and dealing in the mercantile. Of course, self-care isn't just taking good care of your body. One of the most important ways you can practice self-care is by managing your mind and paying attention to your thoughts and what you need for mental relaxation and revitalization.

If you reflect on the Ingalls family's lifestyle, you'll see a pattern that incorporated much-needed downtime more seamlessly than we do today. No alarm clocks, for starters. And whenever they could, the family sat down together for meals and gathered around for stories and fiddle time in the evenings. Typically, Sundays were a church-sanctioned day of rest, a weekly ritual that gave them all time to be still and recuperate. They may not have known (or admitted) it, but with these practices, they were incorporating self-care.

In the "Dance at Grandpa's" chapter of *Little House in the Big Woods*, the whole Ingalls clan donned their best party clothes and cut loose, laughing and dancing the night away. Charles's brother George, whom everyone called a "wild man," challenged his mother to a "jig off," and she whooped the pants right off him! That Ingalls family knew how to split a log *and* cut a rug!

Although your job probably requires less physical work than the frontier folks' did, you still might struggle with taking needed downtime—and you have way more options for letting off steam! If you don't make yourself a priority, you can't be fully present for anything for anyone else. Why not look to your favorite prairie family for inspiration on how to balance your life's wagon wheels to ensure a smoother ride?

Hack #1:
GET OUTSIDE

Mind Your Mother Nature

SOME OLD-FASHIONED THINGS LIKE FRESH AIR
AND SUNSHINE ARE HARD TO BEAT.
—LAURA INGALLS WILDER
FARM JOURNALIST: WRITING FROM THE OZARKS

Mother Nature is amazing, isn't she? Every season she gives you something new to experience and enjoy, even if you have to travel to different climes to discover it all. Charles Ingalls and the gang didn't have to make time to commune with nature; it was part of their everyday lives. Farmers worked in it, kids played in it, and everyone absorbed the fresh air, exercise, and vitamin D that makes us feel alive.

Sadly, it's all too easy to overlook Mother Nature when we're cooped up in front of a screen all day. Without realizing it, days can go by without getting a breath of fresh outdoor air.

> THE GRASS GREW GREEN AGAIN AND
> THE WOODS WERE FULL OF WILDFLOWERS.
> **—LAURA INGALLS WILDER**
> *LITTLE HOUSE IN THE BIG WOODS*

Charles's farming kept him outside most of the day. And when he worked at the mill or was on a job hunt, his outdoor walking gave him plenty of fresh air and a cardio workout. Most pioneer labor was outdoors and physical; along with being farmers, settlers were primarily hunters, trappers, carpenters, or loggers—or all of the above.

> While you're enjoying the fresh air on your walk, freshen up your outdoor surroundings, too! Bring a bag and collect trash and recyclables along the way.

Nature heals in countless ways. It's an antidote for stress, as it physically lowers blood pressure and enhances immune system functioning. What's been coined *forest bathing*—spending time surrounded by trees—exposes you to plant compounds that can increase the number and activity of disease-fighting white blood cells. Being in nature lowers anxiety by reducing stress-related hormones and increasing self-esteem. Even symptoms of attention deficit disorder and aggression lessen in natural environments.

Pioneer settlers naturally combined their indoor and outdoor time each day. Doc Baker walked or rode in his open-air carriage to see patients when he wasn't treating them in his office. Women's chores included everything from washing dishes to hanging laundry, so they were constantly moving between workspaces. With a little creative thinking, you, too, can easily add more outdoor time to your day. If you're sitting at a computer at home, move it outside on your porch, deck, or nearby park when the temperatures allow. Find a coffee shop to work from and walk or ride your bike there. Take walks before you clock in or out or on your lunch breaks. When others take a ten-minute smoke break, take a non-smoke one. Can't get away from your desk or work area? Take a moment to gaze out a nearby window and appreciate the magical changes that happen each season. Look into the middle or far distance and watch the flowers bud, the leaves change color, or the magic of the first snowfall.

Explore the programs that your town or city has to offer; many communities offer fun experiences (nature walks, bird counts, historical tours, community cleanup days) that will get you outside and discovering something new.

When you're not working, getting outside can be as simple as taking a walk in your neighborhood or finding a new trail or area to explore. Did you know that walking not only helps to relax your mind but also boosts your creative thinking? This movement requires the work of both the right and left hemi-spheres of the brain and increases blood flow that helps to stimulate it.

For more outdoor leisure time, read your book on a bench by the lake or socialize outside with friends across a picnic blanket. Go a step further by camping. If that's too extreme, consider some form of "glamping," or if you can swing it, rent a cabin with running water and electricity. Remember, if Harriet Oleson could traipse through the woods to a camp-site toting a full tea service, there's no reason you can't get out there for some one-on-one time with Mother Nature in some manner.

....

YES, THERE WAS A TIME WHEN THE OUTDOORS WAS MY LIFE.
OH, I USED TO BE VERY ATHLETIC. I GUESS YOU CAN TELL THAT BY
NELLIE AND WILLIE. WELL, YOU KNOW, THEY GET IT FROM ME.
—HARRIET OLESON
SEASON 2 • EPISODE 9 • "THE CAMP-OUT"
(UM, SURE THING, HARRIET)

....

If you live in an area with especially cold temps, don't use that as an excuse. There's no such thing as bad weather, only bad clothing. The Ingalls family didn't sport puffy vests, but they wore layers—knitted gloves, scarves, socks, hats, and animal fur to protect themselves against the sometimes-frigid temps. Bodies have an incredible ability to acclimate quickly, especially if you're dressed properly.

On the aforementioned infamous Ingalls-Oleson camping trip, poor Willie made a rash decision when he picked the wrong leaves for his class project. If he'd only remembered the age-old rhyme "Leaves of three, let it be," he wouldn't have picked bunches of poison ivy and been itchin' to go home.

For those of you in wintry states, grab your inner child and take them sledding down a hill. Have a snowball fight with some friends or throw on some ice skates at a frozen pond. Try out snowshoes and pretend you're Pa, making your way through the snowy expanse, taking in the sights and brisk air.

In pioneer times, warm potatoes or yams were not only for the belly but also for pockets as a resourceful way for settlers to keep their hands warm.

Whether you're walking in the woods, relaxing by the ocean, strolling your city streets, or lying among the tall grass of the prairie, taking in the beauty and wonder of the great outdoors can improve your mental and physical health and provide connection with the wide world around you. It feels peaceful and humbling to remember that each one of us is just a small part of the grand collective.

Unpack the Hack

Walking supports and encourages what is known as *divergent thinking*: a thought process that generates creative ideas by exploring many different possibilities and solutions. The next time you need a brainstorming session for work or a creative project, go out for a walk and get inspired!

Hack #2:
SPEND TIME ALONE

Be Your Own Best Friend

WELL, EVERYBODY LIKES TO HAVE A DAY ALL TO HERSELF
ONCE IN A WHILE. JUST TO THINK AND RELAX.
—CAROLINE INGALLS
SEASON 2 • EPISODE 15 • "A MATTER OF FAITH"

It's hard to beat cherished moments with your loved ones and friends, but even the most outgoing extrovert needs time alone to replenish their soul in a way that no one else can. After all, you are your own best friend. Half Pint was a perfect example. She was gregarious and genuinely enjoyed time with friends, new and old. She was also the first one to grab her fishing pole and head off to her favorite pond, all by herself. More than likely, she intended to have fun and catch some fish for supper, but in doing so, she also had time to reflect, think, relax, and do a whole lot of nothing. Doesn't that sound glorious?

> In season 6, episode 21, Nels Oleson finally had enough and left his home, store, and demanding family because he needed some alone time (a.k.a. self-care). And who could fault him?

Even if you feel like you can't get enough time with your loved ones, it's still essential to prioritize *your* solo needs. When you are surrounded by those who demand your time and attention (coworkers, significant others, kids), you often give up your desires without being aware of it. You simply fall into the schedules and recreational choices of those around you.

> Provide yourself a better chance of getting regular quiet time by downloading one of the mindfulness phone apps with a timer. Imagine Pa's reaction to that: "What is this sorcery?!"

With busy work schedules, it can feel difficult to find some Zen time. Toiling away in the field was grueling work for Charles, but also meditative. Doing something for himself and seeing his progress every day, being physically active, and having quiet time alone reminded him of his purpose and cleared his mind when he was struggling.

How can you make sure you're getting some quiet, meditative time for yourself during your busy workday? Walking away from your tasks for a few minutes to take some deep breaths in a quiet space prioritizes your mental health. You might think this kind of thing would make you feel unproductive or worry that it could cut too much into your hectic schedule; however, those are the very reasons it should be a priority. The busier you are, the more solo moments you need.

You may find that you process a range of feelings during reflection time. After Charles's mother died, he had to ride back to the Big Woods to talk his stubborn father into returning to Walnut Grove with him. You can bet that Charles "Never Met a Tear He Didn't Like" Ingalls spent the long journey grieving, replaying memories of his mother, and strategizing how he'd bring his pa home.

Remember when Doc Baker decided to leave his practice and become a farmer because he thought it'd be more relaxing? The only thoughts he wound up pondering were about how he'd made the worst decision of his life—and maybe trying to remember where he put the key to the clinic's morphine cabinet.

Being alone can force you to look at yourself, and sometimes that feels uncomfortable or scary. You may find you start to feel sad for no specific reason. Try to embrace whatever you're feeling and look at the time as an opportunity; discomfort is a sure sign that some inner work could be helpful. Facing those parts of yourself and working through them with honesty and kindness may do wonders for your mental health and overall well-being.

Alone time also gives you a chance to noodle over situations that have been sitting in the cheap seats while you dealt with your life's more pressing day-to-day details. Schedule time to noodle! Should you finally take the quilt-making class? Does it make sense to go back to school? Quit your job? Leave that relationship? Should you audition for a role in a cheesy horror film?

Michael Landon starred in the 1957 cult classic film *I Was a Teenage Werewolf*. In 1987, he satirized that role in the *Highway to Heaven* Halloween episode "I Was a Middle-Aged Werewolf."

You don't have to leave your home to enjoy some alone time. Whether you're sneaking in half an hour or an entire "you" day, spend it doing things that feel personally luxurious: Read, take a bubble bath, journal, bake, brainstorm, meditate, or simply watch your favorite rom-com. Take a break from your phone if you can. You'll thank us later.

If you share a home with a partner, a roommate, or a passel of kids, instruct them to give you some space. Whenever you can, take advantage of an empty house or apartment. Ignore chores or work and focus on yourself, if only for a short time.

Unpack the Hack

Get proactive and put short spurts of alone time on your calendar. Whether it be ten minutes every day or an entire afternoon once a week, make hanging out with yourself a priority. In fact, take yourself on a date! Pick an evening, day, or lunch hour and do something you would normally not choose to do but have wanted to. Visit a museum, go roller-skating, sit under a tree and watch the world go by. Block out your alone time on the calendar as you would making plans with anyone else. Try to do this as often as you are able.

Self-care is not selfish. From work to play and everything in between, check in with yourself regularly. Make your well-being a priority, as your physical and mental health are essential to living a satisfying life. If you can't be first in the bathwater, Pa recommends a nice scrub in Plum Creek. Bonus: You can check off your outdoor time as well!

Hack #3:
ASK FOR HELP

Count on Your Harvest of Friends

IT'S THE PEOPLE THAT ARE DIFFERENT THAT MOVE MOUNTAINS.
—REVEREND ALDEN
SEASON 4 • EPISODE 1 • "CASTOFFS"

Part of self-care is being able to ask for and accept help when you need it. You might feel that it's a sign of weakness, but it can take a lot of strength to admit you could use some assistance. Allowing someone else to lend a hand *is* helping yourself.

Charles often looked past his pride and reached out for help. You saw this in the season 1 episode of *Little House* "A Harvest of Friends." At first, Charles had too much pride to accept help from others, but when he became hurt, he had no choice. Before he cracked his ribs (Michael Landon's first good excuse to be shirtless), he was helping all sorts of people in need, even to the detriment of his own well-being.

Charles wasn't the only one who put others first. His best buddies Isaiah Edwards and Jonathan Garvey didn't think twice about lending a calloused hand, either. Mr. Sprague the banker, however, refused to be charmed by Pa's eye twinkle and solid reputation, and denied him a much-needed loan. Well, Ebenezer Sprague was a horse's ass, and you're going to run into those from time to time. The point is, Charles *asked*—the answer's always no if you don't ask.

LAURA: How do banks make money if they just give it to other folks?

MARY: Interest.

LAURA: Sure, I'm interested. That's why I asked.

—Season 2 • Episode 9 • "Ebenezer Sprague"

Caroline wasn't above asking for assistance, either. When the men were away and the crops needed harvesting, she recruited a group of women who came together and took care of business——and they were happy to do so. In later episodes, Ma shared her cooking expertise to help poor, inexperienced

Nellie at the restaurant. She probably felt proud that her gifts were appreciated when she wasn't tempted to whack Nellie over the head with a cast-iron skillet. In general, settling pioneers didn't have a lot of choice but to ask for and help one another as they shared valuable information, resources, and the muscle that was required to build homes, barns, and buildings. (Remember the barn raising?)

Wendy McClure, author of *The Wilder Life: My Adventures in the Lost World of Little House on the Prairie*, wrote that Nellie's character composite of three real bullies in Laura Ingalls Wilder's life was "some kind of Frankenstein assembled from assorted bitch parts."

Help isn't always a "doing" task. Sometimes emotional or moral support is what's needed. Be an accountability buddy with someone and check in with each other regularly. Buddies share goals (big or small), offer support and alternative perspectives, and encourage each other to keep on track.

Keep in mind that most people enjoy helping. Think of the times you've lent a hand. It usually gives you a boost of confidence when others request your expertise and know-how. When you help someone else, it's a reminder that you're needed, useful, and appreciated. There is deep satisfaction in knowing you are making someone else's life easier. Why would you deny someone else that fantastic feeling?

If you find yourself reluctant to ask for help, try looking at it from someone else's perspective; envision that person asking you for help in the same situation. How would you feel? You'd probably jump right in. The more you ask for help when you need it and see the benefits for you and the giver, the easier asking will get. And if you're still feeling funny about it, offer to pay someone for their help or barter a trade. Ma's homemade bread would surely have been a welcome exchange.

Unpack the Hack

Be proactive! Bake some treats (or buy them from your favorite door-to-door cookie salesperson) and freeze them for those times you may need to ask something of your neighbor; you'll be prepared with an offering to thank them for their help.

Hack #4:
SEEK BALANCE

Slice Your Pie into Equal Pieces

LIFE WAS NOT INTENDED TO BE SIMPLY A ROUND OF WORK,
NO MATTER HOW INTERESTING AND IMPORTANT THAT WORK
MAY BE. A MOMENT'S PAUSE TO WATCH THE GLORY OF
A SUNRISE OR A SUNSET IS SOUL-SATISFYING, WHILE A BIRD'S
SONG WILL SET THE STEPS TO MUSIC ALL DAY LONG.
—LAURA INGALLS WILDER
FARM JOURNALIST: WRITINGS FROM THE OZARKS

The Ingalls family knew that to take good care of yourself, you need a mix of work and play. The whole hardworking town tried their best to attend the traveling circus, fairs, and Founder's Day festivities. They knew that time spent away from the wheat field and the four log walls of their homes would ultimately give them a much-needed recharge, and in turn, better equip them to resume the hard work of their daily lives.

> There is such a thing as too much work. In "Fight, Team, Fight," Coach Ellerbee obsessively trained the Walnut Grove football team at the expense of alienating his own family and causing the players to fall behind in their schoolwork and homelife. As expected, this behavior didn't help anyone, especially not the team; they ended the season with two wins and six losses. A little balance would have gone a long way.

What does balance look like? It's different for everyone. You may find that working Monday through Friday, leaving the weekend for a mix of chores and rest, is what's right for you. Or maybe you're a midweek-break kind of person who feels better after decompressing on a Wednesday or Thursday night. What matters is that you feel fulfilled, but not overloaded, in all areas of your life.

As you're finding balance, pay close attention to your thoughts and your body. Are you constantly worrying about deadlines or thinking about work and responsibilities even when you're taking a breather? Does your body often feel stiff and achy from tension and anxiety? Most people go through periods of stress, and sometimes that can't be avoided. But if you're noticing mental and physical symptoms as a result, it's definitely time to plan a break. Sit down with your calendar and get mindful of your work-life balance. Do you see play-times in your current schedule? As you think about each day, where can you pencil in a spot of time for yourself? When we write things down, we tend to prioritize them.

Looking for ways to get out and give yourself a break? Keep yourself on top of events happening in your area by subscribing to emails from organizations and venues and following them on social media. Do it right now. Never miss another outdoor market or tractor pull again!

Don't forget to let coworkers, family, and friends know when you need downtime. This can be challenging, especially if you're a people pleaser. You may think you're going to disappoint your friends and family if you decline an invitation . . . and sometimes you will. But most likely they will understand if you need to skip '80s dance night this time around, like, totally. With a healthy work-rest-play balance, you're going to be more fun to be around when you are ready to get your boogie on.

Alternatively, if you're a homebody who'd rather clean an outhouse than spend an evening whoopin' it up in public, creating a social balance is still healthy. Perhaps ask one friend to join you for tea, see a movie, or just go for a glorious walk. You don't have to booze it up at happy hour with a crowd of extroverts to feel balanced. You do you.

> Doc Baker did a great job incorporating some social time during his house calls, as he was often asked to stay for coffee and treats!

Unpack the Hack

Creating balance starts with weighing your current load. Write down your detailed plans for the week. How many hours are you working, and how many are spent in play? If exercise is something you want to add to your life, what is the trail hiking–couch potato ratio? When you're trying to eat more fresh vegetables, how often do those show up on your plate each day?

When you take account of it all, it's easy to see where some things may not be well balanced. Come up with a strategy to tip those scales in your favor.

Hack #5:
TAME YOUR WORRY

Climb Out of the Pressure Cooker

I SUPPOSE THAT EVERYTHING IS JUST THE WAY IT SHOULD BE. UNTIL
WE HEAR DIFFERENT, THERE'S NO POINT IN BORROWING TROUBLE.
—GRACE SNIDER
SEASON 3 • EPISODE 17 • "TO LIVE WITH FEAR, PART I"

You were worried this hack was coming, weren't you? But seriously, worry can overtake us faster than a screaming Nellie racing down a hill in an out-of-control wheelchair (see season 3, episode 2).

Pioneers spent a lot of their time living with the unknown. Caroline was always worried when Charles left home to work a long-term job. To be fair, he usually chose the jobs that involved explosives or working from the top of telephone towers. Bad weather caused excessive stress among farming communities—a single storm could wipe out food security for a year. And what of Charles and Caroline, pacing the floors, worried for Mary's future after she lost her sight? *Walnut Grove 56080* could have been a gripping reality show.

WHERE A LIGHT CAN'T LIVE, I KNOW I CAN'T.
—LAURA INGALLS WILDER
LITTLE HOUSE ON THE PRAIRIE

Everyday life may be easier today, but some things never change; human beings will find countless ways to worry. Honestly, life gives us plenty to get anxious about, and we are physiologically wired to do so. Did you know that most of our thoughts are negative? You can blame your amygdala, a structure of cells that hangs out at the center of your brain. It does the important job of emotionally coding memories, but it also takes on the role of an overprotective mother, nagging and scaring us to keep out of harm's way.

The next time a person or situation causes worry, stop and ask yourself if your belief is demonstrably true. Can you find absolute evidence of it? Do you know for sure that you won't get the job? Can you say with complete certainty that last night's date isn't going to call you? You often look for evidence to prove your worrisome belief, but there's usually just as much—if not more—evidence to disprove it.

It's also all too common to aim negative thinking at yourself. When you look in the mirror, what does that voice in your head tell you? Often, it's a torrent of negativity, things you would never say to anyone else. Sadly, this voice is often loud enough to drown out your confidence and keep you second-guessing everything.

Katherine MacGregor (Harriet Oleson) was frustrated with the lack of meaty roles she'd been offered and was worried she'd have to quit acting. Shortly before she was hired for the part of Mrs. Harriet Oleson on *Little House on the Prairie*, she worked at an art gallery.

Well, this voice often lies. It's trying to protect you, but you usually don't need protection from hypothetical harm. Too much time and energy are spent worrying about the future and what may or may not happen. And if the thing you're fixated on does happen, you've worried twice! Additionally, fretting can bring on high blood pressure, chest pain, and a myriad of other symptoms. How can you jig to the fiddle if you're not feeling tip-top?

Stones, beads, and other talismans have been known to calm worry. Some people carry them in their pockets or rub them to self-soothe. Placing the item on your desk or another area where it catches your eye could also do the trick.

So how do you combat worrying? Remind yourself that you only have so much control over what the future may bring. You can be as prepared as possible and things still may go awry. Alternately, things may take an upturn in a way you never expected. A quick trick to quiet worries about the future is to close your eyes and bring your focus to the current moment, which is usually the only short bit of time you can control.

Pa Ingalls sure did sweat, but he tried hard not to sweat the small stuff. For the most part, he did a pretty good job. With some dedication and intention, we can get there, too.

Unpack the Hack

The usual methods, such as deep breathing, meditation, and happy distractions are helpful, but combine those with the work of going to the source of the issue as well.

Think about what is causing you distress at that moment and ask yourself why. Give yourself an actual answer. Typically, this first response will be very broad. Then ask a *why* question around that response. Continue this why/statement/reply until you get to the actual root of the distress. It may take you a few layers in, but often you'll realize that what you're worried about is broader or more specific than what you first identified. Sometimes your ultimate answer will make you feel silly about worrying in the first place! This process allows you to get more of a concrete reason for your worry and gives you something specific to work with.

Hack #6:
CULTIVATE JOY

Stop and Smell the Prairie Flowers

> A GOOD LAUGH OVERCOMES MORE DIFFICULTIES AND DISSIPATES
> MORE DARK CLOUDS THAN ANY OTHER ONE THING.
> **—LAURA INGALLS WILDER**
> *FARM JOURNALIST: WRITINGS FROM THE OZARKS*

Finding ways to fully savor your life is a surefire way to care for yourself. Who doesn't want to drink from the well of happiness? Just make sure you don't fall down that well—Pa's on a lumber run to Mankato.

> NELLIE'S POOR; SHE HAS NO HAPPINESS INSIDE.
> **—OLGA NORDSTROM**
> SEASON I • EPISODE 7 • "TOWN PARTY–COUNTRY PARTY"

Are you enjoying your life? Not merely getting through each day but finding daily joy? Letting your life slip into autopilot can steer you into territory that feels mundane and relatively joyless. We may live a lot longer than our pioneer friends did, but life is still too short to not get the most out of every day.

Despite the hardships, you saw the Ingalls family with more smiles than frowns. They often shared work with others not only to lighten the load but also to partake in some good company and laughter. They planned picnics and socials. Even when things were especially tough, they allowed themselves some small treats. How many times did we hear or read Caroline say, "Oh, Charles, you shouldn't have." Charles understood that life was meant to be enjoyed, even if it did entail spending some of that cash on the barrel a little frivolously once in a while.

> NOTHING LASTS FOREVER UNLESS YOU'RE IN SYNDICATION.
> **—ALISON ARNGRIM**
> *CONFESSIONS OF A PRAIRIE BITCH*

The pioneers saw the days of their lives as precious commodities, not wanting to waste a minute. How can you do the same? Here are some ideas:

+ Be mindful of every day—when you pay attention to the present, you become more intentional.
+ Try something new—learning a new hobby or taking a class for fun expands your options for future enjoyment.
+ Hang out with people who make you laugh—do the people you choose to spend time with bring you joy?
+ Don't take yourself too seriously—find time to let off some steam, get silly, and give yourself a break. Find humor in your blunders; we all make them.
+ When you take your daily walk, tune in to your senses. What do you hear? See? Smell?

✦ Revisit the hacks in this chapter—get your alone time, hang out with Mother Nature, ask for help when you need it, seek balance, and pay attention to your thoughts and how they affect your overall well-being.

Unpack the Hack

Take your vision board to the next level and create a joy journal. Grab a notebook or journal (with pretty prairie flowers on the cover?), old magazines, a glue stick, markers, and some scissors. Look through magazines with the sole thought of *What brings me joy?* Cut out images and words that make your heart twinkle and glue them onto the pages of your journal. Add to it weekly, monthly, or even daily. When you are feeling down or want to give your joy meter a boost, review the pages of your beautiful book. You could even spread the joy and invite friends to a happy hour "brew and glue" gathering.

Prairie Challenge:
TAKE A SOLO EXPEDITION

In episode 23 of the show's first season, "To See the World," schoolmate Johnny Johnson got "tired of reading about far-away places." He wanted to experience them for himself, with no one else tagging along.

There is something to be said about getting away all by your wonderful self. Road trip to somewhere you've wanted to visit or hop on a plane to a new or favorite destination.

There are so many benefits to a solo adventure!

+ Self-confidence is one of the biggest takeaways—not only from planning the trip itself but also creating your schedule and exploring all on your own. Going outside your comfort zone and figuring out challenges that may pop up along the way are huge for your self-esteem.

+ You get to be selfish in the best of ways. Whether you want to plant your butt on the beach or a park bench the entire time or stay active taking in the sights, you only have to answer to yourself.

+ You learn a lot about who you are when you're away from the influence of others. How often do you think about what you like, what you love to do, or how you process things? A solo getaway creates the opportunity for fewer interruptions and deep introspection.

+ Physically surrounding yourself with new sights, smells, and activities not only broadens your learning horizons but offers the chance to openly dream and scheme in a new environment. New stimuli do wonders for your creativity.

Getting away with your best friend (ahem, that's you) provides a chance to see yourself in the world as you are. We realize that even if all you can manage is a day trip nearby, this can still feel very scary! Have a backup plan at the ready if you feel the need to get back home before your original return time.

CHAPTER 8

HACK YOUR
RESOURCEFULNESS

THINK OUTSIDE THE BREAD BOX

EVERYTHING FROM THE LITTLE HOUSE WAS IN
THE WAGON, EXCEPT THE BEDS AND TABLES AND CHAIRS.
THEY DID NOT NEED TO TAKE THESE,
BECAUSE PA COULD ALWAYS MAKE NEW ONES.
—LAURA INGALLS WILDER
LITTLE HOUSE ON THE PRAIRIE

C an you imagine making all your furniture? Here you are, feeling mighty proud of yourself for success-fully mastering those darn IKEA instructions, and there was Pa Ingalls, who not only built his entire house but also used the extra wood to make *all* the furniture that went inside. He probably didn't have any leftover mystery screws, either.

> Charles Ingalls made a lot of his own tools, even the bullets for his gun. Not one to waste anything, he gathered the small lead shavings that fell from shaping the bullets and saved them to create more.

The pioneer life was an extremely challenging one, and resourcefully devising clever ways to overcome difficulties was a requirement for survival. The Ingalls family had to prepare themselves as best they could for whatever hardships might be around the bend, and what they didn't have available to them, they had to make, borrow, or do without.

> Hardship can spur ingenuity. In 1795, the French emperor Napoleon offered a reward to anyone who could devise a way to preserve his army's food. So we can thank him for the process of canning—the heating, boiling, and sealing of food in airtight glass jars that keep it from spoiling.

Take the pioneer mantra of "make, borrow, or do without" and see how it can benefit your home, food, clothing, playtime, friendships, and community. Being half as clever as Charles and Caroline sure sounds like a recipe for success . . .

and hey, you never know when making a wagon wheel from scratch may come in handy.

> Resourcefulness sure was required in the *Little House on the Prairie* makeup trailer. At one point, Melissa Gilbert (Laura) and Alison Arngrim (Nellie) wore braces, which were not period appropriate. The makeup artists covered the braces with white candle wax in the morning and then they'd have to remove it at the end of the day. What a mess!

Hack #1:
HONE YOUR HOUSEKEEPING

Home Is Where the Smart Is

Running your own *Little House* can be overwhelming, time-consuming, and expensive. It may seem like you're stuck in a never-ending cycle of buying cleaning supplies, beauty products, household goods, and gadgets. If you want to become more mindful and resourceful about how you're managing your home, start by looking to your favorite pioneer family.

> In *On the Banks of Plum Creek*, the Ingalls family lived in a dugout sod house with an earthen floor. Can you imagine the never-ending task of keeping that place clean?

Ma was nothing but resourceful when it came to cooking, cleaning, and overall chores. Emulating Caroline Ingalls might feel daunting, but it doesn't take much for you to scale back a bit and rethink what you use and how you use it. In fact, many everyday items you already have can be used to create homemade products that are easy to use, gentle on your wallet, and result in fewer plastic bottles in landfills. A simple online search will give you more than enough recipes and how-to videos to tackle any chore.

Vinegar is a valuable overall cleanser, and its acidity helps to remove lime and scale buildup that results from hard water. Baking soda cleans and freshens, and kosher salt is a great abrasive to scour greasy stove grates and cast-iron pans. A 2:1 mixture of regular olive oil and lemon juice makes a perfect polish for woods, and some cream of tartar mixed with water or lemon juice can remove stains from dishes and brighten up grout.

But before you start making your own products, stretch your dollars and use less by being mindful of how much of your existing products you use.

+ You only need about a tablespoon of laundry detergent to wash a regular-size load. If you still see suds at the end of the cycle, use less detergent.
+ For those of you with short hair, a nickel-size dollop of shampoo will do ya. Medium-length hair only needs a

quarter-size amount, and if you are lucky enough to have a long, luxurious Mary Ingalls–style head of hair, maybe a half-dollar. Work the shampoo in for a minute or two to get the most out of it.

✦ To conserve cleaning spray, spritz the cloth, not the surface.

✦ When preparing food, use only the prep space you need, leaving you with fewer surfaces to clean.

Have you suddenly run out of dishwashing detergent or want a less expensive alternative? Just add three drops of liquid dishwashing soap in the soap slot of your dishwasher and fill the rest with baking soda. Close the lid, run your load, and open your dishwasher to clean dishes for less!

Toss-away items can have multiple uses. The basic practice of rinsing and reusing makes a difference in the way you simplify your resources.

✦ After use with items not prone to salmonella or other bacteria, rinse those zippered storage bags with dish soap and allow them to air-dry or wipe them out with a towel. Better yet, invest in silicone or other reusable sandwich or storage bags.

✦ Give washable cloth napkins and diapers a try (just remember which is which!) or see if you can make the swap from paper towels to multiuse bamboo ones. You'll save money and be less wasteful.

+ Rinse and repurpose juice or other large bottles for storing popcorn, beans, rice, pasta, or any dry goods.

Black coffee was known as "barefooted" to pioneers. They derided weak coffee as dehorned belly-wash or brown gargle. In a pinch, pioneer women roasted, ground, and brewed seed wheat to make a coffee substitute known as Sin and Misery; it was considered a sin to burn the wheat, and misery to drink it.

Composting spent tea and coffee is a great idea, but here are a few more ways to up your coffee and tea resourcefulness game:

+ Before you toss those filtered grounds, look up recipes for using them in a homemade facial scrub, as an abrasive cleaner, or to hide furniture scratches. Recipes abound.

+ Some plants share your love of joe! Acid-loving plants, such as hydrangeas, rhododendrons, holly, or roses, for example, would welcome some of your used grounds mixed in with their soil.

+ Washing dishes *can* be your cup of tea. When added to some water, used tea bags (tea leaves, not herbal) can be placed in a pan with stubborn sticky food to loosen the mess overnight for easy scrubbing in the morning.

✦ Soothe minor rashes and bugbites with cooled tea bags. Cooled bags can also reduce under-eye circles and puffiness—this especially comes in handy after a sob-fest from watching your favorite *Little House* episode.

These household solutions may not seem like much, but even the smallest change can make you more mindful of how you use your resources.

Unpack the Hack

Simple vinegar is a great cleanser, but sometimes you want to use something a little more pleasing to the nose. It's easy to be thrifty and resourceful by making your own scented house-hold cleaner. In an empty, clean spray bottle, add one part vinegar, a lemon or lime rind, and a sprig of your favorite fresh herb. Rosemary, lavender, and sage work well, but don't limit yourself; create your own scent combos!

Shake the bottle and let it sit for about a week to give your mixture a chance to infuse. The lemon or lime rind helps boost the cleaning power; just make sure whatever you're spraying won't become damaged by acidic cleaners. Don't stop at cleaning. Feel free to spritz your herb-forward spray into the air for a clean, fresh smell.

HACK THE HACK: Head out to a favorite store and pick up one of the many green concentrated options available, add water, and spray away!

Hack #2:
STRETCH YOUR PANTRY

Eat with Your Mind Open

> EVERYTHING MUST BE SAVED, NOTHING WASTED
> OF ALL THE SUMMER'S BOUNTY. EVEN THE APPLE CORES
> WERE SAVED FOR MAKING VINEGAR, AND A BUNDLE
> OF OAT-STRAW WAS SOAKING IN A TUB ON THE BACK PORCH.
> **—LAURA INGALLS WILDER**
> *FARMER BOY*

Yearning to get back to simpler times or just to cut costs, many people are rediscovering their love for cooking and baking. It is satisfying to make your own meals; it's cheaper, and many benefits come from the extra effort, especially when you use fresh ingredients and control how much salt or sugar you add. Bonus: More chances to flaunt your best apron-y fashion.

In addition to the health benefits of eating more mindfully, simple resourcefulness can easily become second nature in your kitchen. Having a grocery or convenience store around every corner is a luxury, as is food delivery nearly 24-7.

Sometimes you forget how much money you could be saving if you employed some good old-fashioned Ingalls intention. They grew, raised, hunted, dried, and canned their food and were conscious of how much they used. Just because the pantry was fully stocked one year didn't guarantee there wouldn't be a weather disaster that would affect the next.

According to the USDA, Americans now waste an estimated 30–40 percent of their food supply. Caroline would probably faint if she saw the bounty of food gathering dust in modern kitchen cabinets. How many times have you ignored what you have on hand and ordered delivery or went traipsing to the store to buy more food? Challenge yourself one night a week to make something edible using a random ignored food item on hand. Get creative and find some fun new recipe for that can of garbanzo beans that's been sitting in the back of your cupboard.

> Make the most of what you have readily available using online recipe generators. They ask for ingredients you have on hand and then offer recipes that you can create using them. Instead of ordering takeout, you save money by using what's already in the fridge and pantry.

You can also save money by making your own tasty spice mixes. Why buy ready-made Italian seasoning when you probably already have basil, oregano, rosemary, parsley, thyme, chili flakes, and garlic powder sitting in your spice rack?

Assembling your own unique concoctions is fun, and you get to control the proportion of each spice.

Not only do we tend to ignore the food we have on hand, but we also toss meal leftovers that could easily be composted. At first thought, saving discarded bits and bobs just so they can rot can seem a bit . . . well, gross, but the benefits are huge. Composting promotes less waste and allows you to add precious nutrients back to the soil. You don't have to be a gardener to take advantage of the resulting rich organic matter; simply adding the dirt to your plants, lawns, and around the base of trees brings added benefit. Organic matter also makes an incredible gift for your friend or neighbor who is obsessed with their lawn and garden! Who knew? If you truly have no use for compost, check your community offerings—in many cities, there are farms and composting companies that will happily arrange for a weekly pickup of your vegetable food waste.

Here's a little Ingalls-style ingenuity for being resourceful with food:

+ The next time you're cracking eggs, use your finger to scrape out the excess white that is left in the shells. Why waste that extra protein?

+ Before you toss all those veggie peels into the compost, set aside some for the freezer. These will add excellent flavor to future homemade vegetable stock.

+ Add the green tops of carrots (or nearly any leftover greens) to your dip or pesto.

- ✦ When life gives you lemon peels . . . dehydrate and grind them to make lemon powder. If you don't have a dehydrator, a low-temp oven will do. The powder adds a lovely bright pop to any dish. You can even add a pinch to your skin-care potions for some extra acne-fighting properties and general brightening.
- ✦ Infuse vodka or any other liquor with fruit or herbs that are about to go bad. An apple-peel infusion is a delicious addition to bourbon and brandy cocktails!
- ✦ Toss your leftover veggies into an omelet or frittata or an Italian-style soup with tomatoey broth and small pasta.

Unpack the Hack

Organize your pantry and refrigerator shelves regularly, and turn all food labels forward. Most perishable goes in front. Any new purchases that you're not going to use right away should go to the back. This not only reminds you of what you already have in your kitchen but also makes these items easier to find. Bonus: No more moldy cheese and rotten, wet remains of cucumber in your vegetable crisper.

Hack #3:
GET CLEVER WITH CLOTHING

Go to the Core of Cottagecore

MA HAD BEEN VERY FASHIONABLE, BEFORE SHE MARRIED PA,
AND A DRESSMAKER HAD MADE HER CLOTHES.
—LAURA INGALLS WILDER
LITTLE HOUSE IN THE BIG WOODS

Cottagecore, the trend that has folks embracing a simpler and often agriculturally inspired life, skill set, mindset, and aesthetic, has come for your closet. Wearing clothing that reminds you of a simpler time can help you feel more grounded and connected to things that matter. Think calicos and soft patterns, plaids and sturdy fabrics, simple lace or ruffles for fancy nights, and (mainly) natural fibers that wash easily and do not require chemical cleaning. With breathable clothes that only get softer with wear, there's an easy-breezy look and feel to prairie garb, and in a fast-moving world full of never-ending chaos, that can feel like a breath of fresh prairie air.

The term *cottagecore* was first used on Tumblr in 2018 to describe the aesthetics of a mood board. The rest is history . . . literally.

Long dresses and bonnets of the late 1800s may have looked feminine and totally adorbs on the Ingalls girls, but they were created to keep the sun off their arms, legs, and faces as they did chores in the yard and the field. The hats they wore for sleeping, "mobcaps," were practical as well—they kept their body heat from escaping on cold winter nights.

Bonnets are synonymous with prairie style. But the fun, colorful fabrics we see today would have only been for young girls; older women wore darker hues.

Men's pants during pioneer times were made of canvas or denim so that they were rugged enough to survive the wear and tear of hard work. Thrifty pants were made of repurposed feed sacks. Can you imagine the chafing and itch?

Whether or not prairie garb is your particular style, wearing clothes you love can add joy to your life—but fashion habits can get expensive. Think like a pioneer, even if you don't dress like one. Don't underestimate the fabulous finds at a thrift or consignment store! Many popular vintage and consignment shops are well curated; you can even find designer frocks at a fraction of the price.

> Wayward accidents weren't the only danger travelers faced in the Old West. To protect their hard-earned money from armed highwaymen, many people wore a money belt. You could say that the first fanny packs were invented by the pioneers.

No matter if you are dropping off your old clothes, picking up some new pieces, or doing a little bit of both—frequenting thrift and consignment shops is a great way to do your part in recycling. Additionally, consider donating your gently used wardrobe pieces to your local shelter to help clothe residents. If you're a weekday suit sort of person, your community likely has a program to get business wear to job applicants in need.

> Ma knew that making a good first impression was important. She invested her time in creating and repurposing dresses for Mary's significant events, such as starting a new job at the school for the blind and reuniting with John Jr. in Chicago.

When you do indulge in new clothing, slow it down a bit. Ask yourself if you can envision wearing the item(s) in three years or in five. Before an online binge gets the better of you, leave your items in the shopping cart an extra day. That way, you'll be more certain you indeed want to make the investment. Another tip is to imagine yourself paying for the purchase in cold hard cash. Counting out the tens and twenties in your head might make you rethink things.

Nellie's blue dress was her "stunt dress"—she had only one duplicate that she could get dirty during her more raucous scenes.

On the show, you saw some high-waters . . . and they weren't always near the creek! Most families had multiple children, which made hand-me-downs the standard. The youngest Ingalls kid probably got the raw end of the deal, wearing heavily patched and repaired clothes. Back then, the only way to make outfits last through multiple kids was to take constant care and repair them. Today, a little of that care will go a long way in keeping your own wardrobe spiffy.

> THE GIRLS WERE RIPPING THEIR OLD DRESSES AND BONNETS, SPONGING AND PRESSING THEM AND SEWING THEM TOGETHER AGAIN OTHER SIDE OUT, TO LOOK LIKE NEW.
> —LAURA INGALLS WILDER
> *FARMER BOY*

You don't have to be a master seamstress to mend minor holes that form in clothes or socks. At the very least, pick up a mini sewing kit and keep it on hand for small repairs that extend the life of your clothing. If you want the full-on Caroline experience, see if your community has sewing classes, or even a sewing machine–lending library, and get a little help for more substantial alterations or repairs. Heck, you might be inspired to make a special new Sunday outfit!

In pioneer days, ironing wasn't just for your Sunday best. Pressing fabrics, and paying particular attention to the seams, would destroy any louse eggs or fleas that were hidden in them, assisting in avoiding infestations.

Unpack the Hack

Feel like your wardrobe could use a refresh, but you don't have much money to spend? Add your personal touch to special items (or pay someone else to do it) and make them feel brand-new or at least a little spiffier.

+ Grab some fabric paint and jazz up an old jean jacket, a pair of tennis shoes, or even an old tote or fabric purse. This doubles as a great way to hide small stains or discolorations! Can you imagine Ma Ingalls fabric-painting a covered wagon on the back of Pa's jacket? And embellishing it with the cheeky phrase "That's How I Roll"?

+ Attach some beads to a piece of braided cord to create a unique hatband for a sun or bucket hat.

+ Buy an inexpensive T-shirt at a craft or thrift store (or repurpose an old one) and get creative with iron-on patches, clothing decals, or whatever tickles your fancy!

+ Hand-stitch a calico fabric patch onto your jeans or some lace trim to your favorite skirt for a little prairie panache. We're partial to cone-flowers, black-eyed Susans, and other native prairie flowers.

Hack #4:
MAKE PLAYTIME PURPOSEFUL

You Don't Need a Pig Bladder

LAURA HAD ONLY A CORNCOB DOLL WRAPPED IN A HANDKERCHIEF,
BUT IT WAS A GOOD DOLL. IT WAS NAMED SUSAN.
IT WASN'T SUSAN'S FAULT THAT SHE WAS ONLY A CORNCOB.
—LAURA INGALLS WILDER
LITTLE HOUSE IN THE BIG WOODS

Resourcefulness extends to playtime, too. In the late 1800s, playtime pleasures were simple but rewarding; pioneers read, reread, and shared favorite books, sat by the fishing hole, played checkers with sliced pieces of dried corncob, and tossed the ol' pigskin. Literally. Sticks and rocks made a game of baseball (and possibly did break a few bones?), and basic craft supplies were transformed into simple yet entertaining toys.

There was no screen time to limit on the prairie, and people were required to use their imagination to invent play. How often do you practice this with your leisure time? It's too easy a habit to flip on Netflix and watch the latest detective drama. Try incorporating a little pioneer ingenuity with your kids, your friends, or neighbors.

Adults enjoy simple fun as well. Do you have old board games or a deck of cards that haven't been touched in years?

Pop some corn, invite some friends, and play a round of Uno, or choose another old game randomly.

Kids can use their imagination and have lots of fun making paper dolls and designing their clothing, turning large empty boxes into time machines, and using tables or chairs and a blanket for makeshift forts. An empty bookcase makes a great Barbie condo, and Ken can throw a backyard barbecue around his pool. (You don't have to tell him that it's your large Tupperware container from the kitchen.)

Don't worry, you don't have to cancel your streaming services and sell your game controllers. Just think about mixing a bit of creativity and mindfulness into your recreational time. BTW, if Walnut Grove would've had internet service, we think Nellie would have been addicted to *Gossip Girl*. Definitely.

Unpack the Hack

It's fair to say we have way more resources than the Ingalls family had on the prairie, but we can still be creative in our recreational time. Instead of your usual downtime routine, challenge yourself to change things up a bit.

✦ Create original music on an app like GarageBand or learn to play that ukulele your uncle brought you from Hawaii.

✦ Write a story, a poem, or even a whole book. Hey! What

about some *Little House* fan fiction? We're all dying to know if Nancy ever found her Percival.

✦ Learn to draw, paint, or knit.

✦ Use a free app to learn a foreign language.

For those readers who enjoy adult beverages, create a *Little House* drinking game / watch party combo. Pick a season and episode out of a hat, then everyone takes a drink when Pa's shirt comes off, sincere tears well in someone's eyes, or Nellie acts like a jerk! Warning: Your guests could wind up "three quilts to the wind" in no time flat.

Hack #5:
GIVE CREATIVE GIFTS

Be in the Present

HERE'S YOUR PRESENT, PA.
YOU'D BETTER LIKE IT, BECAUSE I MADE IT.
—MARY INGALLS
SEASON I • EPISODE 15 • "CHRISTMAS AT PLUM CREEK"

Gift giving is a practice that most people enjoy but often becomes a stressful measure of their worth. How much should you spend? How much *can* you spend? Will you find the perfect thing? What will most impress the recipient? What if they already have a pickle fork? There is so much pressure to buy the latest and greatest that it's easy to forget the sentiment behind giving someone a gift in the first place.

Around the holidays, we often go on autopilot, hastily running around buying the gifts on our list just so we can get back to the other items on our agenda. Where is the thought? Where is the enjoyment? Where is the resourcefulness? Christmas and birthdays at the Ingalls home always included thoughtful gifts that were knitted, sewn, or built. Try doing less but meaning more.

> Onion skins can be used to dye yarn green like Laura did when she made the scarf for Pa in the "Christmas at Plum Creek" episode.

Knitting, crocheting, and embroidering are on the rise again. These days, it's not uncommon to see groups of twentysomethings hanging out in a coffee shop with their knitting bags or embroidery hoops emblazoned with funny and irreverent sayings. Ma or Alice Garvey never created racy gifts like that, but they could stitch a kick-ass blossom on a dish towel.

> Consider learning one of the "lost crafts." Buy a beginner kit online or at craft stores with all the supplies and easy instructions you need for a single project. Embellish your gift with something that makes it personal.

Being resourceful doesn't necessarily mean you have to make something with your hands. In "As Long as We're Together, Part 2" from season 5, Charles's crabby boss Mr. Standish wouldn't give him an advance so he could buy a fancy hat for Mary's birthday. He secretly sold his fiddle to buy the hat, but Mary caught wind and bought the fiddle back for Pa. We're not suggesting you sell your fiddle, but if you happen to have an old Nintendo console collecting dust, think about selling it to put toward your gift fund.

Homemade cards are extra special, and there is no need to be an expert artist to create them. Even selecting and printing pictures and phrases to assemble into a collage can illustrate the perfect sentiment at a fraction of the cost, and it's bound to be more personal! A homemade valentine positively screams, "I love you."

And don't forget the possibility that your gift of time may be just what the recipient needs or wants. Offer to paint their worn fence or help them sort through items for a garage sale. Take a friend out for a movie or plan a film marathon at home complete with yummy treats!

Whether you save up to buy those perfect earrings, knit a scarf, bake cookies, offer your time and skills, or plan a grown-up playdate—there are plenty of resourceful ways to put more of yourself into any kind of gift.

Unpack the Hack

Set a goal of making one homemade gift for a birthday or holiday. It can be small and simple (Shrinky Dinks earrings for a friend) or you can think big (a crocheted onesie for your partner), but don't give up; follow the project to the end! If you're not a crafty person, you could regift those things you received but never used. Or save them for a white elephant party.

Hack #6:
TRADE AND SHARE WITH FRIENDS AND NEIGHBORS

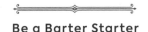

Be a Barter Starter

> MR. EDWARDS HAD INSISTED THAT PA BORROW THE NAILS
> FOR THE ROOF. "THAT'S WHAT I CALL A GOOD NEIGHBOR!"
> PA SAID WHEN HE TOLD MA ABOUT IT.
> **—LAURA INGALLS WILDER**
> *LITTLE HOUSE ON THE PRAIRIE*

When the Ingalls family left the Big Woods, their first stop was the mercantile, where they traded furs for supplies they needed for their journey. The regular practice of sharing and bartering items and services with friends and neighbors has dwindled. Wouldn't it be nice if you could walk into a hardware store and offer a plate of banana muffins in exchange for a package of three-inch nails?

The basic tools required by every pioneer were a gun, ammunition, powder, fishhooks and line, traps, an axe, a spade, and a hoe. With these tools, a pioneer and his neighbors could build, hunt, plant crops, and gather food.

Charles regularly found himself bartering for products and services. In one episode, he needed a plow and seed, but his pockets were empty. He offered to build a roof in three weeks in exchange for the much-needed farming supplies. He also swapped his worn-out horses for Pat (Pet in the book series) and Patty, two strong ones who'd better help them move across the Midwest.

When 1800s farmers lost money because of a bad crop, the local mercantile would extend them credit for their purchases. Their debt was usually payable in part with eggs, butter, and other items the shopkeeper could resell.

Look to your friends and neighbors to borrow or barter, but also search online marketplaces for used goods to purchase, and don't be afraid to ask for barter options there, either. Someone wouldn't have posted an item if they weren't looking to get rid of it. Back in Walnut Grove, patients short on cash regularly paid Doc Baker in pies, apples, and chickens. At one point, he had more feathers than a showgirl!

Speaking of borrowing, a song featured in the "Top Hand" episode of 1971's *Bonanza* (also starring Michael Landon) became the much-loved theme of *Little House on the Prairie*. Musical composer David Rose won Emmy Awards for both series.

Before you buy that tool or household good, check your local library or maker organization to see if they have a tool-lending library. Additionally, many communities have "Buy Nothing" groups and movements, or a Freecycle or Trash Nothing web presence. If you don't find one in your area, consider creating your own group. Even something so simple as pet-sitting swaps can help save money and strengthen community bonds . . . and more animal friends mean more opportunities to make tiny holiday hats as gifts! Resourcefulness also comes in handy when you're thinking bigger than tools, hobbies, and interests. Perhaps you're considering a new life path or endeavor; don't forget to look to the people around you for job inspiration. If you know someone who is doing something you'd like to do, reach out and ask questions! Most people love to feel like an expert and will be happy to share what they know. And if you're admiring someone's work from afar, follow them on social media, buy their books, and borrow from their process to make it your own.

Unpack the Hack

Ask your neighbors what kind of tools or yard equipment they'd be willing to share. Adding yours to the list, create a document with this information, along with contact details, to distribute as a reference in your neighborhood (get permission from everyone, of course). The next time anyone needs something for a home project, they'll know where they can borrow, not buy!

Unlike the Ingalls family, your modern life doesn't depend on resourcefulness; however, you can use pioneer inspiration for simple, clever ideas to do more with less. You don't need to share bathwater with your family, but you could whip up some homemade soap that saves money and leaves you smelling fresh as a field of wildflowers.

Prairie Challenge:
GETTING TO THE CORE OF RESOURCEFULNESS!

Pa's Slow Cooker
Wild Turkey Caramel Apple Butter

YIELD: 4–5 CUPS*

Apple butter is a delicious, comforting condiment that Caroline would have made back in her day. And because so many *Little House* tell-all books share the details of Michael Landon's love for on-set Wild Turkey tippling, we thought you'd enjoy our version of a recipe that even squeaky-clean Pa would have enjoyed!

This no-peel slow cooker recipe is easy, and it comes with an extra bonus; leaving the peels on means less waste and more nutrients, which was the way of pioneer-era folks. This is a great way to use extra apples before they go bad—or even bruised or soft ones!

Don't worry, the alcohol will burn off as the apple butter cooks; what remains is a flavor that's richer and more complex than the plain recipe. Experiment with skipping altogether if you prefer, or add the equivalent amount of cider.

Apple butter is tasty on toast or a sandwich, spooned into your morning oatmeal, mashed into sweet potatoes, or as an unexpected flavor boost to cake, soup, or even roasted veggie recipes!

Although any apple will work well, using a mixture of different varieties results in the best flavor.

6 pounds apples (cubed, cores and stems removed)

1 cup sugar

1 cup brown sugar

2 teaspoons fresh lemon juice

2 teaspoons ground cinnamon

¾ teaspoon ground allspice

½ teaspoon ground nutmeg

½ teaspoon ground cloves

½ teaspoon salt

¾ cup Wild Turkey bourbon

½ cup caramel liquor (we used Smirnoff Kissed Caramel vodka, which is as sweet as Pa himself!)

INSTRUCTIONS:

Add the cubed apples to a large slow cooker and cover with the remainder of the ingredients. Cover and cook on HIGH for 4 hours; do not stir.

Remove the lid. Mash the apples a little with a fork or potato masher and then carefully pour the mixture into a large blender or use an immersion blender directly in the pot. Blend until completely smooth. If you used a traditional blender, add the mixture back into the slow cooker.

Cook on HIGH for another 4 to 5 hours until thickened, with the cover slightly ajar. Stir about every 30 minutes.

Allow to cool before storing.

Your yield may vary depending on how long you cook your apple butter, and the longer you cook it, the thicker it will be. Look for a medium caramel color for good spreading consistency.

CHAPTER 9

HACK YOUR SUSTAINABILITY

HUG A TREE

SHE LIKED THE ENORMOUS SKY AND THE WINDS,
AND THE LAND THAT YOU COULDN'T SEE TO THE END OF.
EVERYTHING WAS SO FREE AND BIG AND SPLENDID.
—LAURA INGALLS WILDER
LITTLE HOUSE ON THE PRAIRIE

aura Ingalls Wilder wrote about the land beautifully. Even if you're a staunch city lover, you can't help but be swept away by the rich, inspiring descriptions of her environment. Throughout her life, she seemed to recognize not only the beauty and wonder that surrounded her but also the privilege to claim a space upon it.

No matter who you are or where you live, you have an impact on the land. For centuries, it was easy for non-Indigenous people to think it was in endless abundance, that everything nature had to offer was there for the taking or mastering, that nature would always replenish what was taken from it. In the mid-1800s in particular, the westward expansion by settlers was part of the idea of Manifest Destiny. Americans like those settlers have had a long and unfortunate history of taking, and those costs of past neglect and pillaging the land are becoming more urgent and obvious with each year. But each one of us can make more conscious decisions to recognize, be thankful for, take better care of, and give back to the environment in hope that it will continue to support us and future generations, in countless ways. You can live in harmony with the earth by the way you choose to run your home, travel, eat, and spend your time.

Washing your hands, face, or even your whole body (brrr!) in cold water naturally closes your pores, sealing in your natural oils. Ma *did* have a spectacular complexion, didn't she?

Pioneers were experts at living sustainably and giving back to the land, primarily because they had no choice. Ma Ingalls didn't wash clothes in cold water because she wanted to save energy, and Mary and Laura didn't walk three miles from Plum Creek to Walnut Grove because Pa was worried about his wagon's emissions.

....

> EVERY MORNING AFTER THAT, BEFORE HE WENT
> TO WORK, PA BROUGHT FISH FROM THE TRAP. HE NEVER TOOK
> MORE THAN THEY NEEDED TO EAT. THE OTHERS HE
> LIFTED OUT OF THE TRAP AND LET SWIM AWAY.
> **—LAURA INGALLS WILDER**
> *ON THE BANKS OF PLUM CREEK*

....

Every apple that wasn't immediately eaten or in a condition to store safely in a cold cellar was canned, used as fertilizer, or fed to animals. Pa mostly utilized fallen timber to build their home and outbuildings. The Ingalls family mainly took only what they needed and were conscious of giving back to the land—they were living a green lifestyle without even knowing there was a name for it! Pa and the gang have a lot to teach, so read on.

Hack #1:
CONSERVE AND PRESERVE

Look for Greener Pastures

First, the good news: You have the power to help the planet with your purchasing decisions! Let's start by thinking like an Ingalls. They would be horrified to see how much money is spent on things that go to waste or end up in a landfill after only a short time. Spending money on things you don't need affects the environment and your wallet. Although today's modern landfills have less of a negative impact (some are even equipped to turn off-gases into reusable energy), they are still a too-frequent source of land, air, and water pollution or contamination. Make the choice to be more mindful of what you purchase and how often. First, ask yourself if you really need to buy something. Can you recycle or repurpose what you already own? Challenge yourself to reduce your personal trash.

We've mentioned how swapping or buying used clothing can help you save money, but do you know just how much it would benefit the environment? The fast-fashion industry is responsible for harmful emissions, polluting the oceans with plastics, and horrible labor abuses, and it's the second-largest consumer of the world's water supply. That secondhand prairie dress is looking better all the time.

You also have the power to affect the planet with the food you put on your plate and with how you make optimal use of what you have. When Pa went hunting in late fall, he dried the meat so it would keep through the winter, allowing him to stay inside when the temperatures were frigid. He also saved the furs because he knew he could trade them for seed when the planting season arrived. Bones made for good soup stock, which could be canned. He didn't waste any part of the animals, hunted only what his family needed, and left the land as untouched as he could.

Did you know there's a real Nellie's Café in Walnut Grove, Minnesota? Just like the restaurant on the show, they serve up good ol'-fashioned comfort food, but you won't find Nellie and Percival making out in the kitchen.

According to the Sierra Club, as much as one-third of food produced in America is wasted. Channel Ma and Pa, and make sure you are getting the most out of your food:

✦ Eat leftovers right away, or freeze them in favor of tossing them. Soup always tastes better the next day, anyway. Always label or date your leftovers, too. Then you have the reminder to eat them within a few days and avoid having to play digestive roulette.

✦ Make homemade stock with veggie peels, scraps, and, if you have it, bones or meat. If you buy a rotisserie chicken, for example, take everything you don't eat and throw it in a pot with any veggies and herbs you have around, and enough water to cover everything by a few inches. Heat at a medium simmer for an hour or two and you'll be rewarded with a delicious, nutritious broth after straining. Soup's on!

- ✦ Compost instead of trash, whenever you can. (See more about this in the coming pages.)
- ✦ Take steps to prolong the life of your produce. Apples, kiwi, bananas, peaches, pears, melons, apricots, avocados, peppers, and tomatoes are some of the fruits that produce the most ethylene, the gas that causes fruit ripening. Storing them separately will prevent them from affecting your other fruits, thus adding days (or longer) to their shelf life. There are also numerous reusable products designed to store perishable fruits and veggies, sometimes adding a week or more to their usable lives.
- ✦ If those luscious berries still look edible (as in *not* moldy) but no longer firm enough to enjoy eating plain, don't toss them! Make some easy refrigerator jam by cooking over low heat until the mixture is a spreadable consistency. Sugar and a squeeze of citrus are optional. Not a jam person? Wash and freeze the fruit and throw it into your next smoothie.
- ✦ Your appliances make a difference, too. Refrigerator technology doubles in efficiency about every ten to fifteen years. Newer fridges use less energy and are designed to keep food fresh for longer. Newfangled technology sometimes pays off!
- ✦ Grow your own vegetables or herbs in your kitchen or backyard garden. If space is at a premium, many vegetables and nearly all herbs have strains that are suited for container gardening. Not only does fresher

LITTLE HOUSE LIFE HACKS

equal tastier, think of all the packaging, shipping, and waste you can eliminate with each plant you grow. And if you have excess bounty, share with your neighbors. They'll love you for it.

✦ When in doubt, ask yourself, "WWCD?" Yes, of course that stands for *What Would Caroline Do?*

"Waste not, want not!" This phrase is accredited to Maria Edgeworth, from her 1897 book, *The Parent's Assistant*. It may be old-fashioned, but it applies itself nicely to the concept of green living.

Cutting down on your red meat and dairy consumption is one of the biggest ways to personally affect our global environment. According to the UN's Food and Agriculture Organization, those products account for about 14.5 percent of global greenhouse gas emissions. Getting most of your protein from plant-based sources is optimal, but if that feels like a challenge, start by incorporating a Meatless Monday.

By eliminating one serving of beef per week, you're saving the equivalent of car emissions from 348 miles per year (Carbon Brief.org).

The reasons and opportunities to live green are many. In addition to curbing spending and food waste, here are some general tips you can run (not drive) with to do your part:

186

+ Use a tub or a stopped sink for washing dishes instead of allowing the water to run while you clean.
+ Plug multiple electric items into one power strip, making it easier to turn off the electricity when you leave home. Turning appliances off rather than leaving them on standby will make a difference in your bill and the environment. And as every modern Pa Ingalls would remind you, "Remember to always turn off lights when you leave a room!"
+ Choose soy or beeswax candles, which are petroleum-free; cotton or hemp wicks are a smart toxic-free consideration, too.
+ Reuse or eliminate single-use items like grocery bags, food storage bags, and napkins.
+ A full freezer uses less energy. If you don't tend to keep a lot of food in your freezer, fill empty jugs with water and keep them frozen. Your freezer and your wallet will thank you.
+ Do as Caroline would have done—hang dry what you can. Your clothes will last longer, and you'll save on utility bills. Bonus if you can hang clothes out in the sunshine; perspiration stains fade at the sight of sunlight. Think of it as nature's gentle bleach, yours (and Isaiah's) for free.
+ Turn your old textiles (sheets, towels, shirts) into cleaning rags. Ma was an expert at repurposing them into curtains, quilts, tablecloths, and even slippers.

- ✦ If a tidy lawn is important to you, consider using a rake on your leaves instead of a gas-powered leaf blower. Noisy, gas-powered blowers spew toxic emissions into the air. Embrace the rake and the little workout it gives you.

- ✦ Switch to natural or homemade pesticides for your lawn and garden. Better yet, research what's native to your area. Did you know that some grasses, when planted in their native regions, only rarely need watering and require mowing no more than once every four to six weeks? Also, let your grass grow a little longer! Keeping grass at four inches will help inhibit weed growth.

- ✦ Save trees! Go paperless for your billing, and cancel any paper subscriptions that you aren't reading. Pa might've skipped his paper copy of the *Inter Ocean* newspaper in favor of the online version if he'd had the chance.

The *Inter Ocean* newspaper was published in Chicago and ran from 1865 to 1914. In *The Long Winter,* Laura Ingalls Wilder wrote about Pa reading that, along with the *St. Paul Pioneer Press.*

- ✦ Make or buy natural, nontoxic cleaners. Everything you pour down the drain ends up in our water supply one way or another.

- ✦ Bike, walk, take public transportation, and carpool as often as possible.

Unpack the Hack

Plan and prepare a healthy meal with one goal in mind: to create little to no food waste. Figure out a use for every little thing. This could mean saving those leftover veggie pieces for soups or broths, freezing leftovers, turning scraps into compost, or repurposing ingredients. Bonus point: Don't use onetime bags while shopping or single-usage storage containers after the meal. Ready, set, go!

Hack #2:
GIVE BACK TO THE LAND

Be the Bee's Knees

THE MEADOWS WERE ROSY-PURPLE WITH THE BLOSSOMS THAT THE BEES LOVED BEST.
—LAURA INGALLS WILDER
FARMER BOY

Give back to the land by connecting with it—make friends with the outdoors, as the settlers did. Like any healthy friendship, kindness to the environment is reciprocal, and your mindfulness nurtures the relationship.

Early pioneers believed that the land itself offered inherent health benefits, and they looked to settle in areas that promoted physical well-being. Additionally, they often blamed the environment for ailments such as constipation or boils. Although they weren't always accurate about the source of these ailments, they were onto something; the settlers seemed to understand that the air they breathed and the soil in which they grew their food had a big effect on their health. Perhaps Harriet Oleson could have blamed her "vapors" on an ill wind?

> Remember when Harriet Oleson claimed she had the vapors? The "injurious exhalations from within the recesses of the body" that were suffered by a book heroine sounded so glamorous— that is, until Doc Baker explained that her diagnosis was only a bad case of gas.

Part of taking care of our land is making sure you're replenishing what you're taking. As we mention in the previous chapter, "Hack Your Resourcefulness," composting is not only a great way to get clever with waste but also giving nutrients right back to the soil from where they originated. Here's how you can get started!

Composting tips:

+ You can set up compost piles directly in the ground or purchase any one of a variety of bins. You can even buy the latest (or used) compost machines that sit on your kitchen counter and break down the waste within hours, odor-free. Wouldn't that have blown Caroline's mind?
+ Selecting the right mix of ingredients is key to an

odor-free compost area or bin. Add two to three parts of carbon-rich "brown" materials—shredded paper, newspaper, cardboard, dried plants or flowers, corncobs (although the Ingalls family would have saved those for the outhouse), dead leaves, napkins—for every one part of the "greens," which include fruit and veggie scraps, bread and grains, coffee grounds, and grass clippings. Make sure to learn what should and should not be included in your scraps.

✦ Even if you don't get a fancy-schmancy machine, care and maintenance of your compost pile is a breeze. Turn the pile anywhere from once a week to once every few weeks, depending on the season. Keep it moist with water; as it breaks down, it should be as damp as a wrung-out sponge. You'll be rewarded with nutrient-rich soil on the bottom.

Plants and trees are nature's air purifiers, as they help provide oxygen and remove chemicals and bacteria from the air we breathe. No wonder the Ingalls family was like a breath of fresh air! Such an easy way to give your health and aesthetics a boost. As our textiles and new furniture have increasing amounts of chemicals from their manufacture or fireproofing, their off-gassing inside our homes also increases. Keep the balance in check by adding houseplants. You don't necessarily have to buy them all, either; many plants can be divided to fill your house or yard—or given to a happy neighbor! A reminder, however: Keeping houseplants can be difficult when you have curious pets that want to eat them. Make sure you check for safe, nontoxic varieties.

> Most indoor plants don't come from cold-weather climates, so use warm water when hydrating your leafy roommate. Bonus: Warm water absorbs into the soil faster than cold does.

Make sure your tree friends stay healthy and happy. Prune them properly, ensure they get enough water, and place mulch around the base to insulate the roots. Replace trees that have been diseased and removed from your homestead, but make sure you're choosing the right tree for your area and planting it in the place that'll give it the best chance to thrive.

> When Pa was finally able to claim his homestead in De Smet, South Dakota, he mentioned what was known as the Timber Culture Act of 1873. Settlers were encouraged to plant ten acres of trees to help cover the bare prairie lands. The timber would provide wood for both fires and buildings, help to act as a windbreak around homes, and provide ecological health benefits for the land.

Consider growing outdoor plants that attract helpful bees and butterflies. Did you know that birds, beetles, and even bats are also considered pollinators? These insects and animals are responsible for assisting a large percentage of the earth's flowering plants to reproduce.

Who could forget the show's opening sequence complete with little Carrie face-planting on her way down the hill? The wildflowers "growing" on that hill were fake ones added for effect, stuck into the ground with wires. Knowing this, that tumble could have been way worse if accompanied by a "wire to the eye" incident.

According to a 2021 U.S. government report, the American honeybee has "declined by 89% in relative abundance and continues to decline toward extinction." This is due to habitat loss, climate change, disease, pesticides, and more. Fewer bees mean less pollination, which affects not just our food supply but entire ecosystem.

Do your part to help bees and other pollinators survive and thrive:

+ Plant pollinator-friendly flowers like lavender, basil, and verbena (shout-out to Miss Beadle). A simple online search will produce an entire list of bee-utiful flowers.
+ Research local programs in your area centered around helping bees and other pollinators. Even major cities have urban bees movements. It's a great way to meet like-minded people, too.

- ✦ Buy honey from local beekeepers. Raw, local honey not only is delicious, but also has vast health benefits. Two tablespoons of this glorious nectar daily is suggested as a natural anti-inflammatory and as an antioxidant supplier. Local honey is also said to help with seasonal allergies!
- ✦ Don't use chemical pesticides. Please don't. They weaken our friends the bees and make them more likely to develop parasites. There is a reason Roundup and its main toxin, glyphosate, have been banned in many countries and hopefully soon, the U.S. Opt for organic alternatives, or make your own solutions. Did you know that corn gluten is a natural herbicide?
- ✦ Birds aren't the only ones who enjoy a nice drink and bath. Create a bee bath with a bowl, some water, and a few rocks for perching (cute!). Like the birds and the bees, Isaiah Edwards liked a nice drink and could always use a good bath.
- ✦ If you are responsible for your lawn, take part in No Mow May! Letting the grass grow tall at the beginning of spring helps flowers bloom to provide nectar to our favorite pollinators. Worried about your neighbors thinking you're lazy? Put a "No Mow May" sign front and center, and it may inspire them to do the same.

And to water these trees, gardens, and flowers? Take advantage of Mother Nature's heavy rain clouds and place a rain barrel at the bottom of your downspout, or simply set it anywhere in your yard. This is an environmentally friendly way to collect and save water for your lawn, garden, and plants. Have more than you can use? Share this with a happy neighbor as well!

> Rain barrels started making their appearance in the 1800s. When the wooden shipping containers could no longer be used, pioneers started setting them out to collect the rain. The hard well water had harsh effects on the settlers' skin and clothing fibers, so they especially appreciated the rainwater.

Unpack the Hack

Give plants as gifts. Choose one that even someone with a black thumb can keep alive, and if it's an indoor variety and they have pets, always make sure it's nontoxic. Not only will they receive an attractive addition to their home decor, they'll also breathe easier . . . and get a green thumbs-up of approval from Pa! Looking to send a bereavement gift? Consider planting trees in memoriam. The Arbor Day Foundation and many other organizations offer affordable gifts of planting trees in someone's name. FYI: Your message doesn't have to be as crass as Victor French's "Eat Shit. Love, Victor" memorial message (see Chapter 1, Hack #1).

GET INVOLVED WITH THE LAND

Dig In

> THERE WAS ONLY THE ENORMOUS, EMPTY PRAIRIE,
> WITH GRASSES BLOWING IN WAVES OF LIGHT AND SHADOW ACROSS
> IT, AND THE GREAT BLUE SKY ABOVE IT, AND BIRDS FLYING UP
> FROM IT AND SINGING WITH JOY BECAUSE THE SUN WAS RISING.
> AND ON THE WHOLE ENORMOUS PRAIRIE, THERE WAS NO SIGN THAT
> ANY OTHER HUMAN BEING HAD EVER BEEN THERE.
> —LAURA INGALLS WILDER
> *LITTLE HOUSE ON THE PRAIRIE*

It must have felt incredible to Laura and her family to find themselves in vast, open areas, with everything they needed to build and farm and not another homestead within sight. You can still find open land that looks and feels untouched, but sadly, you don't have to go far to find litter.

Allow us to trash-talk a little here. A bit of discarded garbage here and there may seem innocuous, but it has more of a negative impact on the overall environment than you might think. In addition to being harmful to animals and wildlife, litter can carry germs and bacteria and can cause disease if it gets into our water sources. Refuse can also clog pipes and sewers, sometimes causing them to burst—not a problem with outhouses.

Plogging is a word. Not to be confused with *clogging*—which is another word for the "jigging" dance that Grandma wowed everyone with in *Little House in the Big Woods*—plogging is the act of picking up trash while you jog. Why are you still sitting there? Start plogging!

First held on April 22, 1970, Earth Day celebrations offer a plethora of options for you to support environmental protection. Most areas organize community events and volunteer opportunities on and around that day to pick up trash, plant trees and flowers, and spread awareness. Even beyond Earth Day, opportunities abound for an organized trash hunt. This can be especially fun when you go with a group!

Another way to get involved with your immediate environment is to patronize your local farmers' market. Can you imagine how happy Caroline would have been if she could have sold her eggs at a community stand versus having to haggle with Harriet? Farmers' markets are in every state and are great places to support farmers directly *and* get fresh food and healthy plants straight from the source. In colder areas, you can find indoor markets that sell seasonal goods. A market is also a great place to pick up homemade items, unique gifts, toiletries, and cleaners that you don't want to make yourself. A hack within a hack!

Plan your own Earth Day activities! For a meaningful bonding experience, involve kids or friends and family. Here are some ideas for a "Build Your Own Earth Day" adventure:

✦ Plant a starter vegetable garden, or break ground on a larger community garden.

✦ Commit to a TV-free day.

✦ Take a hike, and bring something to pick up trash with along the way.

✦ Build a compost bin.

✦ Make tea or cocktails using fresh herbs.

✦ Plant wildflowers local to your area.

✦ Make a bee bath or birdbath.

✦ Commit to keeping these ideas in mind all year long.

Unpack the Hack

Plant a vegetable or two (or five). If the temperatures get cold where you live, create a small kitchen garden using pots or little window boxes. Mini indoor gardens are also perfect for those who live in apartments or other small spaces—classrooms or offices, too! If veggies seem like a lot to handle, choose an herb that tickles your fancy. Wear some cute overalls if you'd like.

If the ideas in this chapter feel overwhelming, you can certainly start small. Whether you decide to live off the grid or simply buy a reusable water bottle, you're taking care of your environment. When you sustain the land, it sustains you. We hope the tips and ideas outlined above as well as the many more at your fingertips will encourage you to regularly do your part.

Overalls were first worn by the British Army in the 1750s, and the first Levi Strauss–refined denim ones were patented in 1873. Overall, they've been a consistently popular piece of clothing that's both fashionable (arguably) and durable.

Pioneer Challenge:
FARM-TO-TABLE FEAST

Help organize or host a meal that includes only farm-to-table foods. You can do this with your family, friends, or even by yourself! If you want to go big, spread the awareness even further by making the meal a potluck and challenge your guests to create a farm-to-table dish that'd rival any Sunday dinner at the Olesons'. Hit up your local farmers' markets, co-ops, and friendly homesteaders for ingredients, and get ready to host your own harvest of friends.

CHAPTER 10

HACK YOUR GRATITUDE

◆━━◆━━◆

SEE YOUR HALF-PINT GLASS AS HALF-FULL

....

AS THE YEARS PASS, I AM COMING MORE AND MORE
TO UNDERSTAND THAT IT IS THE COMMON, EVERYDAY
BLESSINGS OF OUR COMMON, EVERYDAY LIVES
FOR WHICH WE SHOULD BE PARTICULARLY GRATEFUL.
—LAURA INGALLS WILDER
WRITINGS TO YOUNG WOMEN FROM LAURA INGALLS WILDER,
VOLUME I: ON WISDOM AND VIRTUES

....

W̲ith today's endless options and amenities, it's
difficult to imagine what pioneer life was truly
like. However, by recalling both the hardships

and ingenuity of the past, we can learn valuable lessons and appreciate what settlers like the Ingalls family went through. There was certainly no shortage of mud, sweat, and tears! In this final chapter, we head back to Walnut Grove to revisit family, community, faith, romance, friendships, work, self-care, resourcefulness, sustainability, and how *Little House on the Prairie* encourages you to feel grateful for each of these areas in your life.

"Where there's a will, there's a way" was said countless times in the *Little House* books and series. Whether they faced droughts, floods, blizzards, locusts, limited supplies, health scares, grief, or Harriet Oleson . . . your favorite pioneer family met it head-on. Their capacity to meet the struggles with this steady mantra and the uncanny ability to stay grateful through it all was remarkable and inspiring.

Continuously on the air since 1974, *Little House on the Prairie*'s binge-viewing spiked in popularity during the 2020 COVID-19 stay-at-home mandate. *New York Times* TV critics highlighted it as "comfort viewing" during this time.

The Ingalls family had a way of focusing on the present, lifting one another's spirits, and keeping the faith that better days were ahead. They didn't wallow (at least not for long) and tried their best not to whine, complain, or lapse into victimhood. Laura and Pa especially looked for the good in everything, and rarely did their morale falter. You may not encounter some of the drastic experiences that the Ingalls family did, but you can learn from their resiliency and gratitude as you proceed through the chapters of *your* life.

THE ATTIC AND THE CELLAR WERE FULL OF GOOD THINGS ONCE MORE, AND LAURA AND MARY HAD STARTED TO MAKE PATCHWORK QUILTS. EVERYTHING WAS BEGINNING TO BE SNUG AND COZY AGAIN.
—LAURA INGALLS WILDER
LITTLE HOUSE IN THE BIG WOODS

Hack #1:
BE GRATEFUL FOR FAMILY

Thankfulness Is Kin-Deep

HOW DO YOU LIKE THAT,
LITTLE HALF-PINT OF SWEET CIDER HALF DRUNK UP?
—PA INGALLS
LITTLE HOUSE IN THE BIG WOODS

There's no doubt that family was an important part of a pioneer's life. They not only appreciated one another's love and support but also counted on each member to physically do their part. If you have that kind of relationship with your family, and you know they have your back when you need them most, that's a big deal.

> Lindsay Greenbush played Carrie more times than her sister, Sidney, whose arm was in a cast several times during the show's run. Thank goodness for twin actors!

Being part of a family isn't always a picnic, but whether you adore spending time with yours or would rather choose your own, family teaches you so much about yourself and how to navigate outside relationships. If you pull back the gingham curtains on Walnut Grove, you'll find multiple reasons to appreciate family.

+ When Mary left for Winoka to teach at the school for the blind, the Ingalls family was ready for a fresh start and wanted their family to be together, so they followed her. Mary was grateful to have everyone close by so that she could depend on them for emotional support. Whether the members of your family are near or miles away, isn't it nice when you can reach out and know they will be there at any time? Well, maybe some relatives are best held at arm's length, but you get the point.

+ Isaiah Edwards was grateful to be an honorary part of the Ingalls family and happy to eventually form another of his own. There are many people who don't have a choice but to find or create their own family and feel grateful when they discover the ones that feel like home.

✦ Charles learned much from his father. He passed down his ability to become a skilled craftsman and farmer, and Charles inherited his hardworking and loving spirit. He seemed to have a good relationship with both his parents, but even if you don't, you can be thankful for them being the reason you exist or for the things they may have taught you and the talents or positive attributes you may have inherited from them that enrich your life. As always, add therapy as needed.

After Laura Ingalls Wilder died in 1957, her daughter, Rose, edited and published *The First Four Years*, the last in the series of the *Little House* books. She based the book on her mother's diary that documented the beginning of her parents' marriage.

✦ The many wayward children who were adopted into Walnut Grove families felt gratitude for their newfound support systems. Whether you've been taken in to join a family or simply for a family meal, you likely know that feeling of gratitude and inclusion. A slice of strawberry-rhubarb pie doesn't hurt, either. Pay it forward.

✦ Jack the dog was a valuable member of the Ingalls family with his affection and ever-present watchdog skills. Kitty helped keep the mice out of a sleeping Pa's hair. Our pets are family, and we probably lose count thinking of the ways we appreciate them and how to show it. (Note from your pet: Treats help.)

Jeffrey, the border collie who played the Ingalls family's second dog, Bandit, lived at Universal Studios.

Unpack the Hack

When you feel angry or annoyed at family members, counter that thought with something you are grateful for . . . even if you must do some deep breathing exercises first. This doesn't or shouldn't erase or excuse bad behavior, but it helps you to appreciate what you can learn from the situation.

Hack #2:
BE GRATEFUL FOR COMMUNITY

Appreciate Thy Neighbor

Like the Ingalls family, sometimes you choose where you live, and sometimes you end up in a place out of necessity. Whether you land somewhere for life or a shorter spell, you can be inspired by the members of the Ingalls family's community. They all looked out for one another, kept one another in the loop of what was going on around them, and together felt a sense of pride in their town. Not everyone got along all the time, but more often than not, they felt like an extended family. Someone was always willing to scoot down to make room on the church pew. Open your hearts and minds to do the same for a community member whenever you can.

✦ Charles reaped that harvest of friends in the very first episode of the show, and he constantly leaned on them for support. Isn't it the best to have helping hands around when you need them most? Remember, asking for help isn't a sign of weakness. Two of the most powerful things we can say are *please* and *thank you*.

Karl Swenson, who played Lars Hanson, the mill owner and one of Charles's good buddies, was cast as Eddie Haskell's father in two 1958 episodes of *Leave It to Beaver*.

✦ Isaiah Edwards showed up almost as soon as the Ingalls family hit the prairie, and he never left their ever-lovin' hearts. Neighbors can easily become friends for life no matter where you end up, and that's a pretty wonderful thing.

✦ Sometimes you get a challenging neighbor like—shall we all say it together?—Harriet Oleson. These personalities can teach you lessons in patience and perspective. You never know what's going on with the people around you; their struggles can account for less-than-stellar behavior.

Knowing this helps you remember compassion, and that's something to be thankful for all on its own.

✦ Communities are not only about connecting but learning and expanding. Little Solomon, immigrant Yuli, and young Spotted Eagle helped the Walnut Grove community open their eyes and their hearts to those who were different from them. Look for those opportunities in your life and hold them in your grateful heart.

✦ Town celebrations and Sunday picnics were just a few of the gatherings that our *Little House* friends enjoyed. Community events are a way to get you connected and feeling grateful for that togetherness—and the food that often comes with it. Who doesn't appreciate a nice bowl of potato salad?

April 23 is National Picnic Day in the United States. Sounds like the perfect time to host a park picnic or a backyard bash, doesn't it? Appreciate and bond with your community over ambrosia salad, dad jokes, and endless games of cornhole!

✦ If they weren't teaming up to find lost children or chipping in for new schoolbooks, the Walnut Grove crew was uniting to chase bullies out of town. (Even peaceful Reverend Alden got hot under the collar over certain injustices!) Banding together to ensure one another's safety and welfare is another way to show appreciation for your community.

Unpack the Hack

> World Gratitude Day began in 1965 in Hawaii and is celebrated
> annually on September 21.

Celebrate a yearly Gratitude Day for your neighbors. Use the official holiday or create your own. Bake a treat, give a plant, or simply leave a heartfelt note or card at their doorsteps, telling them how grateful you are to have them around. Others just might start doing the same, and before you know it, you could have a loving community that feels appreciated and compelled to be part of the friendly collective.

Hack #3:
BE GRATEFUL FOR FAITH

Keep a Kernel of Hope

"THIS EARTHLY LIFE IS A BATTLE," SAID MA. "IF IT ISN'T
ONE THING TO CONTEND WITH, IT'S ANOTHER. IT ALWAYS
HAS BEEN SO, AND IT ALWAYS WILL BE. THE SOONER
YOU MAKE UP YOUR MIND TO THAT, THE BETTER OFF YOU ARE,
AND MORE THANKFUL FOR YOUR PLEASURES."
—**LAURA INGALLS WILDER**
LITTLE TOWN ON THE PRAIRIE

We've shared ways you can find and keep faith, and how faith and belief were integral to the Ingalls family's lives. Many *Little House* characters inspire you to lean on that mindset to plow through life's hardships. Faith in yourself, others, or something spiritual helps to replace worry and negativity with positivity, acceptance, and peace. Find comfort and gratitude in whatever you rely on to help you through difficult moments and support you as you work toward a rich and fulfilling life.

✦ While it's true that not every member of the *Little House* community was open-minded about others' beliefs, the show didn't shy away from the welcoming message that we all have unique faiths, and they all matter. Say a little thanks for having that freedom of faith.

✦ Faith was regularly tested on the screen and the pages; Charles wanted to give up on things more than once, Jonathan Garvey felt hopeless after losing his wife, and poor Mary had more troubles than any teenager in the history of after-school specials. Your favorite prairie characters showed you that faith can be renewed when you look for sources of comfort, be it friends and family, a higher power, or oneself.

Michael Landon added the character of Albert to the show as a tribute to Albert Muscatele, the son of close friends, who died in a tragic accident. What a beautiful and purposeful way for Mr. Landon to process that grief.

✦ Having faith in yourself and your abilities helps you continue to experience growth. There were many instances when your prairie pals wanted to throw their hands up, but they persevered and often discovered new ways to push through their adversities. This gave them the confidence to keep trying. Whatever would have happened if Laura gave up on her Manly? We shudder to think!

✦ Laura's words expressed how she found her faith refreshed and renewed with the beauty that surrounded her. She saw that hope could always be found in a new day filled with the gift of sunshine, prairie winds, and new opportunities, not to mention her good old-fashioned gumption. Even if you don't see it right away, or it shows up differently than how you'd imagined, have faith that things will work out one way or another. When you have faith that you can wake up each morning to a fresh new start—that's something to be grateful for.

Unpack the Hack

When was the last time you started your day with a thought about just how fortunate you are to rise and shine, even when you're not feeling particularly sunny? Consider that thought before you step out of bed to start your day. Keep a photo or another special item on your bedside table as a reminder that each day is a gift and a renewed opportunity for you to feel faith.

Hack #4:
BE GRATEFUL FOR ROMANCE

Appreciate a Shared Bowl of Popcorn

In *Little House*'s prime-time television form, there was no lack of romance behind closed cabin doors; okay, maybe it was more an air of *tolerance* above the mercantile. Romance is tricky territory that's best navigated with care and gratitude, through smooth *and* rocky terrain. Ma and Pa Ingalls were the most visible example of a grateful give-and-take relationship on the prairie, but even Harriet and Nels had their moments.

> **HARRIET:** I just love you so much, Nels Oleson!
>
> **NELS:** I know that.
>
> **HARRIET:** Do you? I don't . . . Well, I just don't know how you put up with me sometimes.
>
> **NELS:** I don't put up with you, Harriet. I love you.
>
> —Season 5 • Episode 23 • "Mortal Mission"

Maybe a partnership isn't your cup of cowboy coffee, and that's just fine . . . but if it is, there's nothing like some old-fashioned pioneer romance tidbits to help us see that love never goes out of style. Most of it revolves around appreciation of your special one.

+ Whether it was "Television Charles" or "Book Charles," the man loved to surprise Caroline with little gifts. In turn, she knew that surprising her man with an apple pie would go straight to his heart! Treats and presents don't have to cost money or be grand to express the sentiment that you're thinking about your loved one. Knowing what your partner loves and enjoys helps you learn ways to express your gratitude for having them in your life. Heck, even remembering to lower the seat cover over the outhouse hole could be a love note of gratitude.

+ Caroline often thanked Charles for his hard work and ability to provide, and he praised her for tirelessly taking care of him, their kids, and the house. It's easy to fall into routines, but stay out of the ruts. Remember to use your words to let your loved ones know how much you appreciate the work they do and the care they give you.

YOU'RE A WONDER, CAROLINE.
—CHARLES INGALLS
THE LONG WINTER

+ In the "Going Home" episode, Charles was ready to sell the farm and move back to the Big Woods. He then realized that he never asked Caroline how she felt about the move. Talking is a big part of communication, but so is listening.

+ There were many trying moments, more so in the books, where either Charles or Caroline started to lose faith. They took turns holding hope for each other. Be grateful for your loved ones that do the same for you in times of need.

Pioneers drank "cowboy coffee" on the trail. It's made by brewing coarse grounds in water and then pouring it after the grounds have settled to the bottom of the pot. Like a French press, only without the press.

Unpack the Hack

Make a card, write a poem, or even pen a song detailing your gratitude for your loved one. It doesn't have to be sappy—have fun with it!

Hack #5:
BE GRATEFUL FOR FRIENDSHIP

Praise Your Prairie Pals

REMEMBER WELL, AND BEAR IN MIND
A CONSTANT FRIEND IS HARD TO FIND
AND WHEN YOU FIND ONE GOOD AND TRUE
CHANGE NOT THE OLD ONE FOR THE NEW.
—LAURA INGALLS WILDER
FARM JOURNALIST: WRITINGS FROM THE OZARKS,
TAKEN FROM AN ANONYMOUS FOLK SONG

Thank goodness for friends! They support and encourage you, make you laugh, and bring joy to your life. *Little House on the*

Prairie's episodes and chapters are filled with relationships that demonstrate the appreciation and value of having and *being* a good friend. They also caution about fair-weather friends who may be a ray of sunshine one day and a full-on grasshopper plague the next. But yes, there are reasons to be grateful for them, too. Grab your slate and make note of these takeaways.

✦ Where would the Ingalls family have been without the rough-yet-lovable Isaiah Edwards? Don't immediately dismiss someone who isn't just like you. You may wind up feeling thankful for what unlikely friendships bring.

✦ Despite the strained friendship between Caroline and Harriet, they found appreciation in each other. As the saying goes, friends are "for a reason or a season." Sometimes you grow apart, and sometimes you reconnect! What you gain and learn from these come-and-go relationships is worth being thankful for. Think about the past, fleeting friendships that enriched your life in some way, and choose to be open to the next one.

HARRIET: Oh, Caroline . . .

CAROLINE: I'll miss you.

HARRIET: Oh, what a funny thing to say. I don't know who's ever going to miss me.

CAROLINE: Well, I am, and I don't know why.

HARRIET: Well, I'll tell you something. I'm going to miss you, too, and I don't know why, either.

—Season 5 • Episode 1 • "As Long as We're Together"

✦ Half Pint had a lot of fun fishing with her friends at the creek. Isn't it great when you have pals who share your interests? Laura didn't take that for granted, and neither should you.

✦ The television Ingalls family lived most of their lives in Walnut Grove, Minnesota. In reality, Pa was a rolling stone, and he moved his family around a lot. Because of this, Laura's best friends were her siblings. Brothers and sisters don't always feel like friends, so we appreciate them all the more when they do. Remember to let them know.

✦ Laura had a knack for sticking up for her friends through thick and thin. Be the kind of friend who has your buddies' backs and appreciate the ones who have yours. Support means more than a well-fitted corset.

✦ We've all had a Nellie or Harriet in our lives. They push your buttons, and it can feel difficult to find an ounce of gratitude toward them. Maybe no one has taken an effort to give them a chance, and you could open a door to a friendship for which you can feel gratitude. If not, appreciate what you learned from the process and feel good about yourself for trying.

Unpack the Hack

Shake things up with a friend mixer. Host an afternoon tea, dinner party, or cocktail hour, and invite pals who don't know one another but might hit it off. You can't help but feel a bit of gratitude watching connections happen within a group of your special people. You might discount inviting an Isaiah Edwards type to a tea party with a group of friends who enjoy needlework and *Masterpiece Theater*, but you never know who might quilt behind closed doors!

The *Little House on the Prairie* book series covers Laura Ingalls Wilder's childhood and adolescence. Between the years 1870 and 1894, the family lived in Wisconsin, Kansas, Minnesota, South Dakota, and Missouri.

Hack #6:
BE GRATEFUL FOR WORK

Harvest More Than a Paycheck

A LOT OF TIMES WE THINK WE DON'T LIKE SOMETHING
UNTIL WE DON'T HAVE IT FOR A WHILE.
—MA INGALLS
SEASON 5 • EPISODE 6 • "THERE'S NO PLACE LIKE HOME, PART 2"

Whether within or away from home, work is probably a big part of your life. Even though you may not enjoy every second of it, you can find reasons to feel gratitude for it.

Grace Snider was employed by Walnut Grove's post office, and, thanks to her, grateful townspeople received their correspondence. Sometimes the news was about an upcoming visit from a friend, and other times it was announcing a death. Whether good news or bad, Grace's work enabled her to assist in its delivery.

The Ingalls family knew that without their hard work, good times and play would not be possible. Work-life balance is something everyone needs to be reminded of from time to time, but the Ingalls family helps you remember how a hard day's labor is something to be thankful for all on its own.

+ As you saw time and time again, work—and, therefore, a way to make a living—wasn't a sure thing for Charles. If it wasn't unpredictable farming, it was the closing of the mill where Charles picked up extra money. Often, he would have to walk for miles, simply hoping whatever rumor of work he heard would not only be true but also be available to him. Even if you don't love your job, this can remind you to be thankful when you have one!

+ In the books, we learn that Laura never actually wanted to be a teacher. Although it felt like satisfying work, she did it mainly to earn extra money to ensure Mary could get to college or to help her family make ends meet. She also enjoyed the ability to treat herself with a fancy hat, complete with feathers. The simple fact is, the money you earn from working not only supports you for your necessities but allows you to buy things that make you happy, give to others, or have experiences that you wouldn't be able to have otherwise.

✦ Pa mainly farmed alone, but he always had friends to pal around with at Hanson's Mill or when he went out of town to work. Caroline's chores at home were undoubtedly more pleasant when her children were there to help. Although some people work for themselves or in solitary shifts, most jobs provide a welcome opportunity for connection that might not have happened otherwise. Many great friendships or relationships grow out of being thrown into a work environment with someone you otherwise wouldn't have crossed paths with.

During its initial run, *Little House on the Prairie* was popular in countries outside the U.S. The actors' hard work paid off at the TP de Oro, Spain, awards: Melissa Sue Anderson and Karen Grassle both won Best Foreign Actress.

✦ Pa was the family's primary breadwinner, and he felt immense pride and gratitude for making sure that food got on the table. Look around you and think about the ways your earnings serve you and anyone else you support. Work can feel overwhelming at times, but overall, it's a gratifying feeling. Alternatively, recognize the people who may help put a roof over your head and that double soy latté in your hand.

✦ Ma was a tidy housekeeper and kept their little house looking spick-and-span. The family appreciated her efforts, and she felt pleased that she could provide her family with a clean, warm house that they were eager to come home to. Housework can sometimes feel like an unpleasant chore, but isn't it a great feeling when it's finished? Express a little gratitude to yourself for making your own cozy nest.

Unpack the Hack

One way to show your work self-gratitude is to give part of your earnings or a windfall to an organization (or person) who inspires you or has positively influenced your life. The energy of giving is powerful and keeps the good vibes flowing for everyone involved. If you can't swing the cash, offer your time or drop off a small donation of cat treats at a local shelter or nonperishable items to a food pantry. It's the act of giving that matters, and this practice will continue to give back to you in the process and include a greater purpose to the work you do for someone else.

Hack #7:
BE GRATEFUL FOR SELF-CARE

Give Yourself a Charles Ingalls–Style Hug

WHY, THERE IS A GREATER OCCASION FOR
THANKFULNESS JUST IN THE UNIMPAIRED POSSESSION
OF ONE OF THE FIVE SENSES THAN THERE WOULD
BE IF SOMEONE LEFT US A FORTUNE.
—LAURA INGALLS WILDER
WRITINGS TO YOUNG WOMEN FROM LAURA INGALLS WILDER,
VOLUME I: ON WISDOM AND VIRTUES

Little House on the Prairie taught us how to be grateful for who we are and what we can do. We saw and read about people with blindness, debilitating sickness, or disabilities, and we were inspired by how they were able to overcome obstacles. They did amazing things and had fulfilling lives. You can't always predict or control things that happen to you, but you can be mindful of how valuable you are and take care of yourself so that you can be the best that you can be.

The pioneers' self-care was often wrapped in joyful times with family, friends, and hobbies. Their hearts swelled as they laughed around the dinner table with company. They were thankful for games and waltzes at church socials. They fed their souls with the peace of sitting by the creek or lying in the prairie grass, gazing at the clouds.

Pioneers sometimes let their hair down with a rousing game of hide-the-thimble. One person (you guessed it) hid a thimble while the others waited outside. Then it was a treasure hunt to find the tiny object. Good times!

Are you someone who acknowledges and appreciates the big and small ways you take care of yourself?

✦ Most pioneers were probably in pretty good shape. Of course, that came from working themselves to the literal bone, not kettlebells and hot yoga. When was the last time you simply felt grateful for your body, no matter what shape or size it is?

✦ Even with their limited resources, it was important to the Ingalls family to stay educated. When the girls couldn't go to school because of weather (you know, another blizzard) or where they were located, they still made time to study at home. They can inspire you to be grateful for the many things you can learn and for your incredible mind.

✦ When you watch or read about the Ingalls family, you notice how, despite their never-ending work, they knew it was important to have some fun. Let that encourage you to simply enjoy yourself and your life, as often as you can! *That's* self-care.

✦ Pioneers experienced a lot of quiet time, which opened their minds to useful and creative thoughts . . . or simply let them enjoy the peace. How much quiet time do you make for yourself, to open your mind to just *be*? Once you'll probably feel grateful for the break.

✦ No matter if you have the luxury of tropical vacations or relish the simple pleasure of sitting on your backyard patio, remember to recognize the time as special and give thanks for your opportunity to experience it. Although the thought of Lars Hanson's well-oiled chest lounging poolside in Puerto Vallarta is pleasing, he probably felt mighty grateful simply sharing the occasional campfire with Charles.

Unpack the Hack

Give yourself a sweet at-home spa treatment with a two-ingredient lip scrub. Combine sugar and honey, and then rub the mixture on your lips to remove dry, flaky skin. You can thank yourself for the self-care by laying a soft-lipped smooch on your favorite human . . . or pet!

Hack #8:
BE GRATEFUL FOR RESOURCEFULNESS

Get Crafty

During the long winter, whether Pa was twisting hay to use for fuel or Caroline was making a lamp with oil, fabric, and a button, the Ingalls family was nothing if not resourceful.

They had little choice but to puzzle things out, as it meant their survival.

> Mary was quite the seamstress and worked part-time for Mrs. Whipple. As part of her compensation, Mary was allowed to use her sewing resources to make Pa a shirt for a Christmas gift. With an endless supply of thank-yous, Mary knew Mrs. Whipple didn't have to help her, and that filled her heart with appreciation.

You're probably using your resourcefulness quite often without realizing it. When you notice yourself solving problems without automatically assuming you're stuck or asking for help from others, stop and give yourself some credit . . . and some gratitude. *Little House* gave us plenty of examples.

+ A little starvation, grief, or even loss of sight wasn't going to stop the Ingalls family. *The Long Winter* alone was a testament to their strength and courage. Can you imagine living in a bare-bones house with five other people, dwindling food and supplies, and temperatures well below zero? Your life challenges may be wildly different from theirs, but let's be thankful that most of us are born with the innate ability to figure things out when we're in crunch time.

+ Pioneers wouldn't have gotten far if they weren't willing to learn from one another. We're fortunate when we find others who are willing and able to teach us skills or model inspiring behavior. Laura appreciated Almanzo's horse-whispering skills as he taught her the basics of equine training, and she taught him that sometimes a horse responds better to the language of a gentle touch.

The genuine Laura Ingalls Wilder refused to say the word "obey" to her husband in her wedding vows, because she didn't want to make a promise she couldn't keep. Almanzo wholeheartedly agreed, making them both very much ahead of their time! (Go, Laura!)

+ If Nels Oleson vouched for you, you were as good as hired. Aren't we fortunate when we can reap the benefits of a good referral from a resourceful friend?

+ All you have to do is read or watch what little everyone had in Laura's day, to appreciate our modern marvels. That's not to say they weren't excited about new systems and technology coming to town. For example, think of how thrilled Harriet was to have gotten her gossipy paws on the newfangled telephone and switchboard. If you're fortunate to have the means, most anything is at your fingertips. You can connect with people all over the world, at any time, and also get what you need to create, build, fix, plant, cook, and travel in ways the settlers could never have imagined. Our means of resourcefulness are constantly changing and renewing. Let's practice a little gratitude for that.

....

IN OUR MAD RUSH FOR PROGRESS AND MODERN
IMPROVEMENTS, LET'S BE SURE WE TAKE ALONG WITH US
ALL THE OLD-FASHIONED THINGS WORTHWHILE.
—LAURA INGALLS WILDER
*WRITINGS TO YOUNG WOMEN FROM LAURA INGALLS WILDER,
VOLUME 2: ON LIFE AS A PIONEER WOMAN*

....

✦ The Ingalls family had a way of holding reverence for all
the resources that were available to them. They hunted
or caught only the animals they needed to survive and
used all the parts. They appreciated the nearby creek
for water to drink and wash with. They recognized their
privilege to have what they did, even when it wasn't
much. Take a moment to do the same.

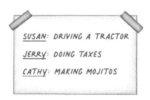

SUSAN: DRIVING A TRACTOR
JERRY: DOING TAXES
CATHY: MAKING MOJITOS

Unpack the Hack

Make a list of your close friends and family, and beside each
name, write something they're good at. Maybe it's math, baking, or gardening. The next time you need help, cross-check
your list for your resources and ask for it . . . and remember
to thank them. While you're at it, reflect on what you're particularly good at so you and your talents can be of assistance
to others.

Hack #9:
BE GRATEFUL FOR THE LAND

Grow Appreciation

THE FUTURE IS IN OUR HANDS TO MAKE IT WHAT WE WILL.
—LAURA INGALLS WILDER
FARM JOURNALIST: WRITINGS FROM THE OZARKS

The environment you live in is so much a part of your life that it's easily taken for granted. The quality of the air you breathe, the water you drink, and the food you eat are all so heavily influenced by how we treat our habitat. When you enjoy fresh, healthy food or water, do you take time to acknowledge their origins? The Ingalls family always said a prayer before mealtime, and you can certainly do that if it feels right. Thank a higher power, thank the land (and the people who originally inhabited it), and thank the animals and crops your meal came from. Take time to appreciate what you receive from the land, and with some *Little House* help, get some inspiration to do your best to keep the environment healthy.

I KNEW THERE WOULD BE RIVERS TO CROSS AND HILLS TO
CLIMB, AND I WAS GLAD, FOR THIS IS A FAIR LAND
AND I REJOICED THAT I WOULD SEE IT.
—LAURA INGALLS
PILOT EPISODE

- The farmers were always thankful for a bountiful crop, and they knew that their ability to grow one depended on a healthy environment. We, too, can remember how to hold reverence for the land and that extra serving of mashed potatoes by being more mindful of how we buy, store, and consume food.

- Much of Laura's writing was admiration of and gratitude for the land around her. She found ways to appreciate not only what the land could provide for her family but also every landscape's unique beauty. Take a cue from Laura and really look around to take in the beauty that surrounds you.

In *The Long Winter*, the Ingalls family would not have survived if it weren't for the wheat they ground (in a small manual coffee grinder!) every single day to bake bread. Laura mentions how hard it was to exist solely on that same thing, day in and day out, but if it weren't for that wheat and that bread, they would have ceased to exist at all.

Unpack the Hack

Show the land your gratitude by planting a tree every year on your birthday (or another special occasion—Arbor Day?). If you don't have a yard of your own or you have enough trees, contact your city and ask how you can donate one. Visit it when you can and thank it for producing oxygen and clean carbon dioxide for you to breathe. Extra credit for hugging it!

> THE TRUE WAY TO LIVE IS TO ENJOY EVERY MOMENT
> AS IT PASSES, AND SURELY IT IS IN THE EVERYDAY THINGS
> AROUND US THAT THE BEAUTY OF LIFE LIES.
> **—LAURA INGALLS WILDER**
> *FARM JOURNALIST: WRITINGS FROM THE OZARKS*

Laura and friends remind us to appreciate our present-day bounty *and* look for gratitude in the small things that sometimes go unnoticed. Her family's life was anything but easy, yet they embraced the simple. This can be hard to do in such a fast-moving world, but it's important to try. When you occasionally slow down, pay attention, and are mindful by appreciating simplicity, you add calmness, peace, and gratitude to your life.

Pioneer Challenge: REMEMBRANCE BOOK

At the beginning of the television series, Laura ruminates many times on what she would write if she had a remembrance book. Why don't you start one of your own? Not just a daily journal but a book about your family and the history of where you lived, the houses where you resided, and why you made the choices you did. List things your family liked to eat and do, your favorite things about communities you were involved with, and anything you think your descendants might find interesting.

You may not pen several best-selling books about your experiences, but this is something you can leave behind that will be a page in the history of your life, your family's life, or both. It may seem like everyday things to you now, but we've seen how much things have changed . . . who knows where your relatives will be in 150 years or so? What a gift it will be for them to have such a detailed glimpse into their past.

AS YOU READ MY STORIES OF LONG AGO, I HOPE YOU WILL REMEMBER THAT THINGS TRULY WORTHWHILE AND THAT WILL GIVE YOU HAPPINESS ARE THE SAME NOW AS THEY WERE THEN. IT IS NOT THE THINGS YOU HAVE THAT MAKE YOU HAPPY. IT IS LOVE AND KINDNESS AND HELPING EACH OTHER AND JUST PLAIN BEING GOOD.
—LAURA INGALLS WILDER

CONCLUSION

A s our world changes and uncertainty sometimes clouds our thoughts, many of us find comfort in simplicity and self-sufficiency. Pioneers like the Ingalls family had a lot of this figured out and left us a well-worn trail as guidance in the *Little House on the Prairie* books and television series. We may not choose to travel by covered wagon or build a log home from the ground up, but with a little of Pa's ingenuity, Ma's resourcefulness, Mary's creativity, and Laura's gumption, we may be able to live more mindfully and still have time to fiddle our faddle with a jig or two round the campfire. And remember . . . don't forget the apple fritters.

ACKNOWLEDGMENTS

Angie's Acknowledgments

Endless gratitude to a latchkey childhood spent in front of the TV or with my nose in a book. I've spent a lifetime being entertained and inspired by Gen X pop culture. I mean, who wasn't mesmerized by Half Pint's sass and Pa's endless integrity (and long, flowing locks!)? Thank you, Laura Ingalls Wilder, for your beautiful reminders that mindfulness and simplicity go a long way in this modern world of ours.

Thank you to Shannon Kelly, our hardworking editor at Running Press. Your enthusiasm, guidance, and encouragement made the process delightfully seamless. And an extra thank-you for wearing your best cottagecore attire to our first video call. #respect

This book wouldn't be what it is without the dedication and support of our literary agent, Sorche Fairbank of Fairbank Literary Representation. Seriously, what *can't* you do? Thank you for believing in us and reminding us that this book can be "even more than what the reader expected." You're the best!

As always, my friends and family (human and feline) are my biggest cheerleaders, particularly my husband, Chris, who gives Manly Wilder a run for his money.

Finally, a wagonload of gratitude to my dear friend and coauthor, Susie Shubert. Our energy and words vibed perfectly together, and I can't imagine sharing this experience with anyone else. Thank you for all the coffee, laughter, and shared journey into the world of Laura Ingalls Wilder. You're the apple to my fritter.

Susie's Acknowledgments

I must start my shared gratitude with a shout-out to my childhood friend and fellow *Little House* fan, Laura (not Ingalls!). She joined me in endless reenactments of the show and the books, always let dark-haired me be Mary, and had a lovely mother who made us our very own prairie nightcaps to fully embody our pioneer roles. I believe that experience in addition to my overall love for the many Gen X feel-good television families like the *Brady Bunch* and the *Partridge Family* led me down this wagon trail to the land of *Little House Life Hacks*.

My return to Walnut Grove would never have been as welcome, cozy, and all-around fun without my coauthor, Angie Bailey. Being able to share this experience together was another wonderful chapter in our twenty-three-year friendship remembrance book! Her endless support, incredible talent, and the ability to always make me laugh made this experience super fun and ridiculously easy. Ang, you're the fritter to my apple.

To our agent, Sorche Fairbank, of Fairbank Literary: Mere written (or spoken!) words could not express how thankful I am that you decided to hop on our wagon and come along for this crazy-enjoyable ride! Your support and kindness have always gone above and beyond.

A big thank-you to editor Shannon Kelly for seeing our vision and running with it straight into the prairie sunset! I am so grateful to you for your energy and enthusiasm!

I'm so thankful to my wonderful friends—you know who you are—and of course, a big hug of heartfelt thanks goes to my husband, Cory, and my kids, Vivian and Sullivan. Our little house wouldn't be the same without your endless love and constant encouragement.

Land Acknowledgment

We would like to acknowledge the original inhabitants of the land on which we reside and have written this book, the past and present Wahpekute group of the Očhéthi Šakówiŋ people. We honor them with respect and gratitude and hope that as you read this book, you recognize and reflect on their sacrifice. A portion of the authors' proceeds of this book will be donated to these Indigenous people, and we encourage you to research your own personal history and lend support as you can.

ABOUT THE AUTHORS

ANGIE BAILEY is a Gen X pop-culture nerd, award-winning writer and humorist, and the author of the *Texts from Mittens* daily cartoon, books, and desk calendars. She shares her life with one witty husband, plus two human and two feline children.

SUSIE SHUBERT helps others navigate their unexpected journeys as a writer and content creator for modernprairie.com, a tarot advisor, and a former graduate of the school of rock. The basis of all that she does is her life coaching certification through Oprah's favorite, Dr. Martha Beck, and the loving support of her husband and two kids.

They both live in Minneapolis.